PICTURE THIS!

APPLIQUÉ PICTORIAL QUILTS—FROM PHOTO TO FABRIC

MARCIA STEIN

Publisher: Amy Marson

Creative Director: Gailen Runge

Acquisitions Editor: Susanne Woods

Editor: Cynthia Bix

Technical Editor: Nanette S. Zeller

Copyeditor/Proofreader: Wordfirm Inc.

Cover Designer: Kristen Yenche

Book Designer: Christina D. Jarumay

Production Coordinator: Zinnia Heinzmann

Production Editor: Julia Cianci

Illustrator: Tim Manibusan

Photography by Christina Carty-Francis and Diane Pedersen of C&T Publishing, Inc., unless otherwise noted

Published by C&T Publishing, Inc., P.O. Box 1456, Lafayette, CA 94549

Library of Congress Cataloging-in-Publication Data

Stein, Marcia.

Picture this! : appliqué pictorial quilts--from photo to fabric / by Marcia Stein.

p. cm.

ISBN 978-1-57120-838-5 (soft cover)

1. Appliqué--Patterns. 2. Quilting--Patterns. 3. Photographs on cloth. 4. Wall hangings I. Title.

TT779.S676 2010

746.44'5--dc22

2010006221

Printed in China

10 9 8 7 6 5 4 3 2 1

DEDICATION

For my parents

ACKNOWLEDGMENTS

Many thanks to the following for their advice and support:

The Tuesday Group That Meets on Monday: Claudia Comay, Diane Kern, Jean Lehman, Chris Renner, and especially Karen Flamme. Thanks for being there.

Susan Cable, willing listener and good friend since sixth grade. Next year's dinners will be all about you!

My sister, Marjorie Collins, always ready with a thoughtful answer from across the pond whenever I needed one.

My wonderful students, who continue to teach me more than I can possibly teach them.

The talented, dedicated team at C&T, and especially my editor, Cynthia Bix, for her sound advice and good humor at every step along the way.

CONTENTS

INTRODUCTION

Are there favorite photos in your closet that you'd like to make into quilts but don't have a clue where to start? Or perhaps you've been making traditional quilts for a long time and are ready to try something new. Maybe you're familiar with machine appliqué but would like to improve your techniques or learn new ones. If any of these apply to you, then read on. I'll show you how to create quilts from your own photographs, even if you don't know how to draw or don't consider yourself to be an artist or photographer.

Before you can begin, you'll need a photograph to work with. If you're at all intimidated by the prospect of making your own photos, don't worry—in this book, you'll find simple shooting strategies and composition tips to make it easier to transform your photos into quilts.

And though many of you may be familiar with using a computer graphics program to print photos directly onto fabric, you may not be aware of other ways in

which these programs can help you with your projects. I will cover how to use a program such as Adobe Photoshop Elements during the design process to help you see small details, determine values, and make transparencies.

Depending on your project and whether you're more interested in product or process, you can choose from several methods of machine appliqué with raw, fused, or turned-under edges. In fact, there's no reason you can't use all three techniques in one quilt, since no one method is always appropriate for every situation.

I've also included several projects so you can practice the techniques presented. I hope you are inspired to expand upon these techniques and move beyond the projects (and perhaps even a bit outside your comfort zone) to create work that is truly your own. I may have given you a road map, but the destination is your own. So let's get started!

START WITH A PHOTO

INSPIRATION IS EVERYWHERE

Find Subjects That Bring You Joy

I've based my quilts on travel photos that encompass a variety of subjects, but there is no reason you can't explore closer to home. The key is to find subjects that excite you, regardless of where you are, because that enthusiasm will carry over to your viewers through your work. You may find inspiration in anything from flowers to buildings to people and pets. If you already know what you love and where to find it, no further decisions are needed before you head out with your camera. But if you don't, here are some ideas to help you get started.

HOBBIES

Hobbies can be a good source of inspiration. If you like to garden, for example, then your backyard flower or vegetable patch might be a good place to start. As you snap the shutter, you may recall how you planted the seeds, watered the sprouts, and watched them grow into the hardy specimens in your viewfinder. Later on, you might think back on those moments as you choose and arrange your fabrics. As you work on your quilt, always remind yourself what it was that made you want to take the photo in the first place, and then concentrate on getting that quality into your work. If it was the way a certain petal curved, make a special effort to ensure that the petal looks just that way in your quilt, and save the artistic license for other areas of the piece that are less meaningful to you.

Original photo

Santa Fe Pickup, 77″ × 54″, Marcia Stein, 1999
Photo by Marcia Stein

A group of flowers doing their best to crowd a chair.

"But I don't garden," you say, "and I don't know how I can turn a pastime such as reading into a quilt." One answer is that the hobbies need not be yours—they can belong to a member of your family, or even strangers. You can use photos of your husband with the big catch from his latest fishing trip, your son sliding into third base, or your daughter tending goal at her soccer game. I've taken photos of classic cars at rod and custom shows, even though automobiles are not a hobby of mine. Sometimes, though, you just get lucky: I saw this one on the highway and caught up with it later in a restaurant parking lot.

Single flowers should have multiple shades of color to avoid the "big blob" look.

A single flower makes a nice subject.

Red-hot hot rod

Many hobbies are based around collections: coins, stamps, clocks, hats, teddy bears, teapots, dolls, bottle caps—the list is endless. You can set up a still life of some of your collectibles, take a photo, and go from there. Sports and other physical activities are also a large hobby category: fishing, dance, tennis, skating, golf, bicycling, surfing, and yoga are among the many options. And if the activity is that of a loved one, you've met the enthusiasm requirement already!

PEOPLE AND PETS

Other good choices are people and pets. For both copyright and privacy reasons, you shouldn't take recognizable photos of strangers, especially children, without permission. This is one reason my quilts often feature people viewed from the back (and because it's easier to do!). If you want to include faces with recognizable features (though that is not covered in this book), take photos of people you know and love, and your feelings will come through in your quilt as well. Otherwise, if you can't resist using a photo with a recognizable stranger whose permission you neglected to obtain, you should change or even eliminate all facial features so they are unrecognizable in your quilt. You might also want to consider making the figure a silhouette.

A boy and his bike

Zoey Blue Eyes, 21″ × 21½″, Julie Banfield, El Cerrito, CA, 2009

Max, 27½″ × 23″, Iva Baker, Novato, CA, 2009

Some of my students have made charming portraits of their beloved cats and dogs. This is another example of how your love for the subject will shine through without any special effort on your part.

MAKE SURE IT'S YOUR OWN VISION

Sometimes, out in the field, photography students are encouraged to look through their instructor's viewfinder. Although I find this educational, I prefer not to drag my tripod over to the exact spot and attempt to replicate the teacher's vision. If it isn't my vision to begin with, I know that I won't be able to execute it well or with enthusiasm, and this will show through in the final product.

NOT EVERYTHING WILL WORK, AND THAT'S OKAY

Depending on your likes and dislikes, not all subjects that appeal to you will be right for your project. For example, the hills of Tuscany are gorgeous, as are the many photos and calendar shots I've seen. But it's not my favorite kind of photography, or quiltmaking for that matter. I prefer close-up photography to landscape work, and I need a bit more color variety to keep my interest for the additional time it takes to make a quilt.

Your photo doesn't have to be perfect to successfully translate into a quilt. In fact, it's not a bad idea to use a photo with some room for improvement, as this can be a good opportunity to demonstrate your artistry and not merely replicate a scene in minute detail.

Be a Tourist in Your Own Town

Sometimes the best way to find a good subject is to pretend to be a tourist in your own town. This can give you fresh ideas, since you're now looking at your environment through the eyes of someone seeing it for the first time. As you walk down familiar streets, you'll notice things you overlooked before, when you weren't actively seeking them out. Suddenly, ornate doors, hanging laundry, and quirky fire hydrants are everywhere you look.

If you still can't figure out where to go and what to shoot, go where the "real" tourists gather and see what interests them. In my case, I might go down to San Francisco's Fisherman's Wharf, Chinatown, or Golden Gate Park. For you, it might be Central Park in New York, The Bean at Chicago's Millennium Park, or Farmers Market in Los Angeles.

But what if you don't live in a town where tourists naturally congregate? Perhaps you reside in a rural area where picturesque barns are plentiful and where horses, cows, and chickens are a part of daily life. This can work to your advantage when it comes to taking good photos, whether at home or on vacation. When I look at the Golden Gate Bridge, for example, I think the subject is so beautiful that I need only point and shoot. Unfortunately, this produces yet another forgettable image of a famous landmark. But when I shoot something prosaic, I pay more attention to composition and other guidelines, resulting in a much more interesting photo. Here's an example from a trip to London.

Run-of-the-mill photo of Big Ben

Shadows provide interest in this otherwise ordinary scene.

TAKE YOUR CAMERA EVERYWHERE

Do as the tourists do and take your camera everywhere. Even better, keep it at the ready so you won't miss out, as I did, if you come upon a lion dance in Chinatown or a Tin Man in full costume strolling through the theater district. The subcompact digital cameras so popular today are perfect for this. Their small memory cards replace the pockets full of film we used to carry, and it doesn't cost anything to take lots of photos.

DON'T GIVE UP THE SHOT

Be persistent when you see a scene that interests you. If you feel at all self-conscious, remember that most people are far too busy worrying about themselves to pay much attention to you.

The first time I saw the Venetian gondoliers that eventually wound up in my quilt *Drumming Up Business* (page 23), they didn't stand still long enough to be photographed. Determined to capture them on film, I lingered nearby, but they never stopped moving. Eventually, they left; undaunted, I began to follow them, but they soon disappeared into a bar. Since it would have looked a little unseemly to follow them into the bar (not to mention the poor lighting conditions), I went on my way. But as luck would have it, when I got back to the square where I'd seen them earlier, there they were again, and I got several nice shots. (Never mind that I let the film sit undeveloped in my camera

for a year!) So it can be worthwhile to revisit the scene and try to get something you missed the first time around, especially with tourist attractions.

Gondoliers in Venice

Give Yourself Assignments

If you find it hard to play tourist, another approach is to give yourself assignments. If you have something in mind and know where to find it (flowers in a nearby garden, for example), so much the better. If not, it might be easier at first to limit yourself to a particular subject or place.

SUBJECT-DRIVEN ASSIGNMENTS

You can concentrate on your chosen subject (e.g., flowers, windows, doorways) and go to different places throughout the day to find more, perhaps resulting in a series. Or you can spend more time on one subject, such as a barn, and shoot it from different angles. Either way, the choice is yours. Just remember, the subject is the driving force; where you go to find it is secondary.

PLACE-DRIVEN ASSIGNMENTS

If you're unable to decide on a subject, think instead of a location where you might find something of interest. You don't need to go far; your own neighborhood is a good place to start. Parades and festivals are perfect, but you can also look for interesting architectural features on the block where you live, people relaxing on benches at the local shopping center, or dogs at play in a nearby park.

SERENDIPITY

Serendipity can also play a role. If you can't come up with an assignment before you leave the house, don't worry! Just head out the door with camera in hand and an open mind. After a while, something will catch your eye, and soon you'll notice more of the same. Almost without realizing it, you'll have created an assignment for yourself, and before you know it, your camera's memory card will be full.

If you like the subject enough, it can become the basis for future assignments. After I did my first quilt of a pickup truck, I started to notice them everywhere I went. I've since done several quilts of old cars and trucks, and now I make a point to look for them on the street. I found this little gem in its native France, but I've since seen enough of them in other places (Santa Fe, San Francisco, and Italy) to produce a series if I want.

Original photo

Deux Chevaux, 22″ × 15″, Marcia Stein, 2001

ONE THING LEADS TO ANOTHER

Here's something that can happen in all three of the above scenarios, provided you remain flexible and keep an open mind.

A bright blue door sparks your interest, so you pick "doors" as an assignment. After a while, you find no other attractive doors, so you decide to look for "blue" instead. Soon you notice a blue umbrella, but then you see no more blue things for a while. It begins to rain heavily, and more people open their umbrellas, so now you decide to look for "umbrellas." This, in turn, can lead you back to thinking about color itself as a subject; a bright yellow umbrella may be the start of a new search for golden flowers, fruits, vegetables, rain slickers, hats, cars, or even school buses.

PEOPLE AS SUBJECTS

People can add interest to your photos, even if you don't think so at first. Initially, I wanted to capture this narrow street in Venice without any people, as in the photo in the top left. But when the gentleman with the umbrella entered the frame, I snapped the shutter again to produce the photo on the right; I think the second image is more successful than the first because of the sense of scale and the additional interest he provides.

Venice street scene

Venice street scene with walker

As with subjects and places, you may want to limit the scope of your assignment—"people" is a pretty broad category. For example, you'll soon discover that older folks and toddlers hold their bodies in more interesting ways than the rest of the population, and they also tend to wear brighter colors. Men in colorful shirts and women in flowered blouses or bathing suits can make wonderful subjects, as can your favorite nephew barreling around the backyard on his tricycle.

My Dad at 90 Years Old—His Best Side!
42½˝ × 45˝, Donna Bachmann,
Pacifica, CA, 2008

Sisters, 16˝ × 21½˝
Elvia Dawson, Temecula, CA, 2009

ENLIST OTHERS IN YOUR SEARCH

The nonquilters on a photo tour of Italy couldn't understand my quest for laundry photos until I showed them what I had done with a similar photo I'd taken in France. Once they saw the original photo, they eagerly sought out laundry for me to photograph. So don't be afraid to enlist the help of others; sometimes people like to participate in your journey almost as much as their own.

Original photo

SORTING THROUGH IT ALL

At the end of the day, you may not think you accomplished much, but once you get home and sift through your images, the benefit of having limited yourself to a certain place or subject will become more obvious. The pattern that emerges may start you down a path of inspiration you never before thought possible. "Who knew I was so attracted to bicycles?" you might think. Who, indeed!

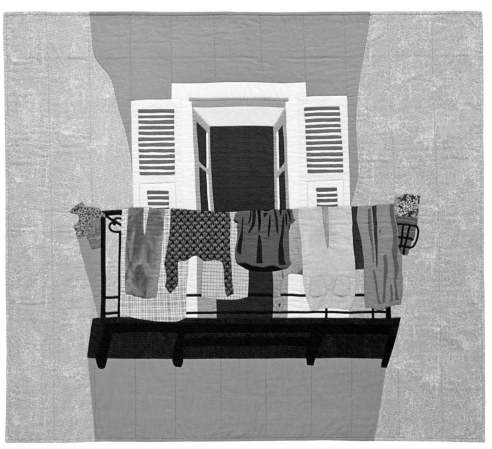

French Laundry, 51″ × 44″, Marcia Stein, 1998

SIMPLE STEPS TO BETTER PHOTOS

Although you can change things you don't like about your photo as you translate it into fabric, working with a reasonably good image is still easier than trying to alter too many things after the fact. My aim in this chapter is not to provide you with a complete photography course, but to familiarize you with some basic concepts and briefly outline a few simple steps you can take to improve your photos. A wealth of information is out there in books and on websites if you decide to explore photography in more depth on your own. You might also enjoy a photography course at your local community college or adult education center. For information on some of your camera's technical features, see Basic Camera Settings (page 20).

Use the Right Camera

I enjoy photography as a hobby and have more cameras than I care to admit. Just as you might have one sewing machine at home and a smaller one that you take to workshops, the same reasoning applies here. If I were going to the wilds of Montana to take in the big skies and record them for posterity, I'd bring my larger single-lens reflex (SLR) camera with interchangeable lenses and a sturdy tripod. If, on the other hand, I'm on my way out for an evening with friends and want to take a few snapshots around the dinner table, a subcompact camera is ideal. If I want a bit more control over my images but still want to keep my equipment reasonably sized, a compact camera will fit the bill.

Left to right: single-lens reflex, compact, and subcompact digital cameras

I assume that most of you use compact or subcompact digital cameras. The good news is that certain basic principles apply to any type of camera you use, be it large or small, digital or film. However, I won't attempt to give you camera-buying advice—technology changes so quickly that any recommendations would be obsolete by the time you read this book.

Secrets to Success

You can improve the quality of your photos and raise them above the level of snapshot with just a few simple changes.

GET UP CLOSE

Have you ever seen a majestic bird and transformed him with your camera into a tiny black dot in the sky? Shooting from too far away is one of the most common mistakes, yet one of the easiest to fix. Simply move in closer to your subject; this lets viewers know right away which element in your photo is the most important. If there's only one important element, you'll leave no doubt if you completely fill the frame with it. (Of course, in the case of the bird, you'll probably need a very long telephoto lens to achieve the desired result.) More often than not, getting closer to your subject will reveal interesting details that make it worth the effort.

This field of flowers is nice enough, but notice the greater impact when the frame is filled with one important element.

Flower field

Single flower in close focus

CHECK THE CORNERS OF YOUR VIEWFINDER

Check the outer edges of your viewfinder or LCD (liquid crystal display) screen for any distracting elements before you press the shutter release. The outer edge is where you're most likely to find the errant candy wrapper, the parked automobile, or the dried-up flower that can spoil your otherwise perfect shot.

In this photo, I was so enchanted by the flowers sticking out through the spokes that I didn't notice the paper and dead leaves strewn about. Clearly, I neglected to follow my own advice; otherwise, I might have tried to remove the offending pieces from view.

Bicycle wheel and attendant debris

A nice feature of digital cameras is that you can immediately see whether your photo has a problem and remedy it on the spot (if your subject hasn't moved). I was still using film in the bicycle wheel example, so I didn't realize there was an issue until it was too late. But if I ever make a quilt from this photo, you can be sure there will be no litter in the final product!

TRY DIFFERENT VIEWPOINTS

Another simple way to improve your photos is to change your viewpoint. This simply means moving around until you see something you like in your viewfinder or LCD screen. But don't just take a few steps to the right or left. Stand on a chair, sit on a bench, lie down on the grass—do whatever it takes to get the shot you want. And don't worry about what others may think as you scurry up and across that park bench!

Viewpoint was a factor when I chose the photo for *Mama's Got a New Set o' Wheels*. Lower viewpoints can add drama to a subject. It was no surprise that I preferred the shot my father took when he was kneeling down, because it magnified the hood and made the car look almost ready to "take off."

Photo from standing viewpoint

Photo from kneeling viewpoint (notice also how this changes the background)

Mama's Got a New Set o' Wheels, 56″ × 38″, Marcia Stein, 2005

Unless you're lucky enough to spot a child perched on a parent's shoulders, your photos of children will be more effective if you get down to their eye level and see the world as they see it.

Changing your viewpoint will also change the background. If a parked car sits in front of that old Victorian house you want to photograph, altering your viewpoint is the only way to eliminate that particular distraction.

A related question to ask yourself is whether the scene in front of you would work better as a horizontal or vertical composition. We tend to shoot more horizontal photos, because that's the way we customarily hold our cameras. But simply turning the camera 90 degrees will allow you to see whether the results would be more satisfactory the "long way." With digital cameras allowing for infinite experimentation, there's no reason not to shoot both ways and decide later which is best.

A vertical orientation was more natural for these flowers.

These flowers look comfortable in a horizontal frame (though if I were to do it over again, I'd blur the background more).

THE RULE OF THIRDS

Your images will be stronger if you follow what is known as the Rule of Thirds (though it's mostly thought of as a guideline). To put this into practice, mentally divide your viewfinder into nine equal sections (like a tic-tac-toe board) and place the important elements of your image at one or more of the four intersections, or at least along a gridline. If your camera has an option to show gridlines in your viewfinder or on your LCD screen, you should take advantage of this feature.

With the grid superimposed on the photograph below, you can see that the flowers and the wall corner extend along a gridline, while the flowers themselves cross one of the focal points as well.

Camera manufacturers tend to put a focusing sensor in the center of the frame, so it's a natural tendency to place your main subject there. But having your subject smack dab in the middle, unless it takes up the entire frame, is just not that interesting for your viewers. Instead, focus on the subject with your shutter halfway down and recompose, keeping the Rule of Thirds in mind. That way, your subject is still in focus but no longer dead center when you release the shutter.

So think about this guideline the next time you're tempted to equally divide water and sky in a sunset scene. If the dramatic sky is what excited you as you looked through your viewfinder, you need to let the rest of us know that by increasing its prominence in the photo. The Rule of Thirds will help show the way and lead your viewers' eyes around the photo.

Original photo

Photo with gridlines

NOTICE THE LIGHT

The thing to remember about light is that it changes all the time. It changes with the weather; it changes with the seasons; it changes with the time of day. (This is one reason not to worry if your fabric doesn't exactly match your photo; if you had squeezed the shutter a minute or two earlier or later, the color might well be different.)

Photographers like to wait for the right light to come along. The light that comes from the side in early morning or late afternoon is warmer and gives some dimension to a scene. But if you're on a whirlwind tour of France, with a guide herding you from one attraction to the next, you don't have the luxury of waiting until late afternoon for the golden cast of the sun to reach the Eiffel Tower. If you find yourself in the harsh light of the midday sun, you can concentrate instead on close-ups or look for interesting shadows in architectural details.

Photographers also like the saturated colors produced in overcast light. While this is good for photography, it can be more difficult to make a quilt look dimensional without obvious shadows.

The saturated colors produced by overcast light attracted me to the laundry in this scene.

The colors aren't as striking in this photo, but the shadows create more depth and would make a more interesting quilt (I also prefer the composition). And I can always change the colors!

You can learn a lot about light by photographing the same scene at different times of day and then studying the results to see which you like best.

HOLD IT STEADY

If everything else is right but you don't hold the camera steady, your blurry results will be underwhelming, even to your mother. Fortunately, there are things you can do to remedy this common problem.

Use a Tripod

Aside from holding the camera steady for you and preventing blurry photos, the tripod helps you slow down, think about composition, and check all the things that might detract from your photo before you squeeze the shutter. Of course it won't help catch your daughter in midair at her soccer game, but when you're shooting the expansive vistas of the Grand Canyon, it's invaluable.

Get the sturdiest tripod you can imagine yourself hauling around. There's nothing worse than watching a lightweight tripod tumble down a windy hillside, taking your expensive camera with it. Other options in a pinch include monopods, beanbags, or mini tripods (especially useful for smaller cameras).

Use Your Body

In the absence of a tripod or other stabilizing equipment, you can brace yourself against a nearby wall, door, or tree.

Stand with your feet apart and your elbows close to your body—don't leave them flapping out there like chicken wings!

Gently squeeze, rather than stab, the shutter release (or use the camera's two-second self-timer so that you're no longer touching the button when the shutter fires).

Take Advantage of Your Camera's Features

If your camera is equipped with image-stabilization technology, you may be able to get away without a tripod in instances when the shot might not be possible otherwise. But remember, image stabilization only compensates for the slight shaking associated with handheld photography; it cannot help you with a moving subject. And for the long exposures required for dusk or nighttime photography, you'll still need a tripod for best results.

Basic Camera Settings

If you get to know your camera controls before going out to take photos, you won't end up fiddling with unfamiliar buttons and dials while a nun in sunglasses breezes past you on roller skates (ask me how I know!).

Even though you probably want to use your camera much the same way you drive your car—without needing to know every detail of its operation—it's still helpful to be aware of a few things that will improve your ability to make good photographs. (Believe it or not, the owner's manual is your friend!)

There's no harm in setting your new camera on fully automatic until you're more comfortable with it. If it has scene settings (for portraits, landscapes, fireworks, and so forth), you may want to use those for a while as well. When you're ready, take the time to learn whatever manual modes your camera offers so that you can increase your control and creativity.

Your goal is to make a proper exposure so that your photo is neither too light nor too dark. Exposure is created through a combination of ISO setting, shutter speed, and aperture.

The ISO (which stands for International Standards Organization) works with the shutter speed and aperture to produce a properly exposed photograph. ISO numbers indicate the sensitivity of digital sensors to light. In a digital camera, you can change the ISO from shot to shot. ISO numbers range anywhere from a low of around 50 to a high of 1600 or more.

As a practical matter, you want to use the lowest ISO you can to get the sharpest photos. The higher the ISO number, the more likely that your picture will be grainy (referred to as "noise" in digital cameras), though there has been much improvement in recent years with higher ISOs.

On the other hand, a higher ISO allows light into the camera faster, so it can come in handy to freeze a fast-moving subject in midair. In a camera that doesn't allow for direct manipulation of shutter speeds and f-stops (see below), increasing the ISO is the easiest way to eliminate blur from action shots. Increasing the ISO may also help you get the shot in a dimly lit museum or church where tripods and flashes are not permitted. Experiment using the same subject and light with different ISO settings, so that you can see the difference.

Shutter speed governs the length of time that light is let into the camera. It works in tandem with aperture and ISO to create the proper exposure for your photo. The shutter speeds on my compact camera range from a low of 15 seconds to a high of 1/2500 second (commonly expressed as 2500). Shutter speeds increase as the numbers go up, so a shutter speed of 250 is faster than a shutter speed of 60.

To capture a sharp image of a fast-moving subject, you'll need a higher shutter speed. So the next time your son is making his big midair catch in center field, use the shutter priority setting on your camera—you choose the shutter speed, and the camera chooses the proper aperture to create a good exposure.

The **aperture** is an adjustable lens opening that controls how much light reaches the digital sensor. Numbers that you can set, called **f-stops**, designate the relative size of the opening and indicate the amount of light allowed through the lens. The higher the number, the smaller the opening, and vice versa. So on an SLR, an aperture of f/2.8 means the opening is much larger, and therefore lets in more light, than an aperture of f/22. (Your highest f-stop on a compact camera is more likely to be around f/8. However, you can still get sharp photos at that aperture, because aperture scales are relative and vary among cameras and lenses.)

Aperture affects **depth of field**, which is the area of a photo that appears sharp both in front of and behind the main focal point. A smaller aperture, such as f/11, will produce greater depth of field than a larger aperture, such as f/3.5. You should use a smaller aperture (larger f-stop number) when you want more of the picture to be in focus (such as a landscape with mountains in the background) and a larger aperture (smaller f-stop number) when you want to selectively focus on an object while blurring its surroundings (often done with flowers). Note, however, that this kind of selective focus is easiest to achieve with an SLR and may not be possible at all with a compact camera because of technical limitations.

My inspiration photo for Point and Shoot (page 24) has a shallow depth of field. This means that the background is softened to the point that you can't really tell what it is, because I was primarily interested in the shirt, which remains sharp in the photo.

Use your camera's aperture priority setting to gain control over depth of field—you choose the aperture, and the camera chooses the appropriate shutter speed. This setting is especially suitable for shooting stationary objects.

White balance: Among your family photos are probably a few tinged with orange because you used daylight film indoors with incandescent lights and without a flash or filter to compensate. Other photos in your collection might have a green cast from fluorescent lights for the same reason.

In digital photography, proper use of the white balance setting will avoid this problem. You can let your camera figure out the proper white balance if you want (the auto setting), or you can choose from among several other settings, such as daylight, cloudy, tungsten, or fluorescent.

WORKING WITH YOUR PHOTOS

Choosing the Right Photo

Now that you've taken some photos of your own, you'll need to pick one as the basis for your quilt. Just as enthusiasm for your subject matter is important when you're out with your camera, you should be equally excited about the image you choose to translate into a quilt. Before you decide on a particular photo, it's a good idea to articulate what it was that made you want to take the photo in the first place—its essence, if you will—and always keep that in mind as you work, to ensure that it remains in the final piece. That way, your enthusiasm will shine through to your viewers.

You may already have photos tucked away in your closet that you can put to use. As you sift through them for possible quilt subjects, remember that it's best to keep it simple for your first effort. Images with high contrast and a single major subject will be easier to work with.

Sometimes it can be hard to make a decision between similar photos, especially when the differences are subtle. For example, here are two photos I took of gondoliers near my hotel on a trip to Venice.

Gondoliers, Photo 1

Gondoliers, Photo 2

As you can see, they are quite similar. So why did I choose to base my quilt *Drumming Up Business* (page 23) on Photo 1 rather than Photo 2? The gondolier on the left looked the same in both photos, but the one on the right had moved a bit from one photo to the next as he spoke with the nearby tourists, and I thought the differences were subtle but significant. In Photo 1, I preferred the position of his left arm and hand, the angle of his hat, and the flow of his ribbons. I also liked the way his left heel was a bit off the ground in that photo, which added movement. However, his right elbow was obscured by the tourist, so I "borrowed" it from Photo 2 when it came time to make my master drawing. I was especially interested in the flow of the stripes and how the end of the sleeve looked, details I couldn't discern from Photo 1. If I didn't have the second photo, I could have made educated guesses about these elements, but as long as I had something I could use as a reference, it made sense to do so. This is one reason it's a good idea to take several photos of your subjects and their surroundings whenever possible.

As for the other fellow, I loved the way his left arm was perched, but I wanted to know what it was resting on so that I could make an informed decision about possible changes. Again, a reference photo I took showed that the wood structure was one of the many bridges dotting the Venetian landscape.

Reference photo showing larger portion of bridge

I chose instead to pretend that his arm was resting on a flower stand, because it gave me an opportunity to add color in that area with a vase of flowers.

Drumming Up Business, 42″ × 62″, Marcia Stein, 2005

Simplifying the Background

Over time, I have found that most designs require simplification when translated into fabric. In my quilts, this most often means changing the background, usually for one or more of the following reasons.

Unavoidable distractions: You can't control the background when you're out shooting in a public place, so random people, cars, and pets can make their way into your viewfinder just as you snap the shutter, no matter how careful you are. In the case of *Gypsy Legs*, where I was in the middle of a parade, I couldn't worry about the extra legs and skirt whirling past me, but I could certainly eliminate them from my quilt.

Original photo

Gypsy Legs, 47″ × 47″, Marcia Stein, 1999

Lack of clarity, color, or interest: Sometimes you'll want to make the background more interesting or colorful, or perhaps you can't quite tell what the background is to begin with. In the photograph for *Point and Shoot*, I deliberately focused on the patchwork shirt and blurred out the background, so it's impossible to tell from the photo what the man was looking at. I substituted a mountain view with flowers at the base, which added some needed color and provided a scenic background that I thought might be worthy of a tourist's attention.

Original photo

Point and Shoot, 27″x 19″, Marcia Stein, 2006

Technical issues: You may want to reproduce an element just as it is in the original design, but perhaps you don't have the right fabric, or maybe your current skills aren't up to the task. Much as I would like to claim that all my decisions to simplify are based on some sort of grand artistic vision, the truth is that sometimes I'm just not able to achieve a good result any other way. For example, I very much wanted to include the background details in *'52 Pickup*—the street with its double yellow line, along with the sidewalk, adobe wall, and stone fence across the way. But no matter what I did, the result lacked dimension, and I finally decided that a plain wall would work just as well and be a good way out of my dilemma.

Original photo

'52 Pickup, 61″ × 42″, Marcia Stein, 2003

Combining Photos

If taking out small distractions, composing a new setting, or eliminating the background won't work, you may want to combine photos. In *Window Shopping*, I wanted to represent the couple as they were in the original photo, but I soon realized that even though I did like some of the background elements, especially the hats, I was unable to include them in a way that didn't detract from the main subjects.

Shop window in Florence, Italy

Original photo

Window Shopping, 34″ × 51″, Marcia Stein, 2007

On the other hand, since it was a shop window, the couple did need to be looking at something. I searched other photos for ideas, came upon one I took of a shop window in Florence, and used it to help change the background of the quilt. (I cover how to do this in Making Changes Along the Way on page 63.)

HELP FROM YOUR COMPUTER

Researching Photo Details

You may decide to work from a photograph in which some of the smaller elements are unclear. If similar photos in your collection are just as ambiguous, you can use the Internet to research those details and reproduce them more accurately in your quilt. For example, when I decided to make a quilt honoring my mother, I chose to work from a black-and-white photograph taken by my father many years earlier. (To see the finished quilt, *Mama's Got a New Set o' Wheels*, turn to page 15.)

Original black-and-white photo

I needed more detail, not to mention color, in order to translate the image into a quilt. Starting my search with family albums, I found a color slide taken the same day, along with a few from other road trips. Even though the slides were somewhat faded and showed the color a bit differently, they helped confirm my general memory of the car.

Color slide taken on a trip to Canada

Resolving Design Issues

Your computer's usefulness does not end with research. You can also use it to help you with design. I use Photoshop Elements, and the examples in this chapter are from that program. However, other programs work similarly.

ENLARGE FOR CLARITY

Sometimes you can't distinguish an object in your photo well enough to draw it accurately. This problem may not even show up until you're hard at work on your master drawing. At any point in the process, you can use a computer graphics program to enlarge the unclear portion of the photo.

You can often solve the issue by zooming in enough on the problem area to identify it on the computer screen. If that doesn't help, crop your photo down to the area of interest and print it out. Even if the resulting photo is pixelated and somewhat unclear, it can still reveal the bits of information you need to know. When I was working on *Point and Shoot* (page 25), I wanted to see how the man's fingers were holding the camera, so I cropped that portion of the original photo to get a better look.

But that still wasn't enough. For example, when I was choosing fabrics, I needed to know if the curved piece on the side of the car in front of the rear wheel was chrome. I suspected it was, even though it wasn't shiny in any of my photos. I went online and found the original sales brochure for the 1954 Chevy, and the drawing made it clear that the curved piece was meant to be chrome. Then I found a reference on another website to "chrome gravel guards" as a feature of the car. So the piece was in fact chrome, but it didn't appear so in my photos because it was reflecting the dull gray of the asphalt. The pieces of the puzzle were starting to fit together, and I was able to choose the appropriate fabric for this piece—a medium gray with a bit of sparkle.

When I had trouble distinguishing the details of the Chevy logo in the "Bel Air" chrome plate on the side of the car, a close-up shot on an auto parts website cleared up the ambiguity, and I was able to portray it correctly. A drawing of the same logo in the sales brochure helped me get the colors right.

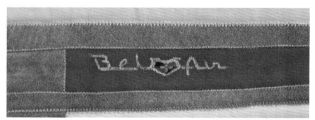

Mama's Got a New Set o' Wheels (detail; full quilt on page 15)

Cropped portion of photo

Even after you enlarge the photo, you still may not be able to tell what the object is. Chances are good that no one else will be able to tell what it is either, so it's usually safe to draw what you see and not worry about it.

POSTERIZE TO DETERMINE VALUES

If you pay attention to light and dark values in your quilts, your subjects will have dimension and look more realistic. Sometimes it's easier to see the different values in black and white than in color. At other times, lightening your image, whether color or black and white, may help you see what lurks in the shadows. This is where Photoshop Elements comes in handy.

> The simplest way to convert a photo to black and white in Photoshop Elements is to select Image > Mode > Grayscale. If that doesn't yield satisfactory results, consult one of the many books or online tutorials available for other methods.

If converting the image to black and white doesn't work, you may want to *posterize* your photo. Simply put, posterizing is a method by which a computer graphics program transforms your image into the number of values you specify. Your goal is to be able to discern values in your photo in the form of shapes that you can translate into fabric.

In Photoshop Elements, select Filter > Adjustments > Posterize. In the Levels window, enter the number of values you want. If you have too many values, the photo starts to resemble the original; too few, and some parts of your subject may disappear altogether. Consider also how easy or difficult each version would be to render in fabric. Don't be afraid to experiment; you'll soon see which number works best for your situation.

Merely changing to black and white didn't help delineate the clothing folds in the inspiration photo for *Window Shopping* (page 26), but posterizing did. (You can also posterize a black-and-white photo.)

Posterized with four values

CREATE YOUR QUILT

THE MASTER DRAWING

To start the journey from photo to quilt, you'll need to enlarge your image to make a master drawing. In addition to using it as your general road map, you'll put your master drawing to use in some or all of the following ways.

Master drawing for *Point and Shoot* (quilt on page 25)

■ Trace it onto freezer paper to make your templates for turn-under appliqué (pages 47–48).

■ Trace the shapes onto the paper side of fusible web (page 55). (**Note:** Your drawing needs to be reversed [mirror image] for this. If you can't see the pencil lines on the reverse side, you can use a lightbox or darken the lines with pencil or a thin Sharpie.)

■ Use it as a guide to create units from your individual pieces (page 59) and as a surface on which to pin your pieces as you baste them into units.

■ Use it as an overlay to help position pieces on your background fabric (page 61).

■ Trace it onto the quilt background or muslin with wax-free transfer paper as another way to help with placement of your pieces (page 61).

Getting from Photo to Drawing

To make your master drawing, you'll need to enlarge your image onto paper the size of your finished quilt. I like to project an inkjet transparency of my photo onto gridded vellum using an overhead projector. I then trace the projected image onto the vellum with a pencil, making changes as necessary. Alternatively, you can do the same thing with an acetate tracing of your photo, which is what I generally have my students do. I describe both methods and the supplies needed in the pages that follow.

If you don't have access to an overhead projector, you can head down to your local copy shop with your acetate drawing to get an enlargement.

> I describe enlarging with an overhead projector because that is my preferred method. However, you are free to use whatever method you like best, whether it's a grid, an opaque projector, a slide projector, or a scanner.

SUPPLIES

- Overhead projector (if you enlarge the photo yourself): Although a somewhat older technology, overhead projectors are still available at large office supply stores and can often be rented or borrowed from your local school or library.

- Vellum (8 × 8 grid, 36″-wide roll, available at art supply stores), butcher paper, freezer paper, or drawing paper to make a full-size master drawing; or, have a local copy shop enlarge your acetate drawing for you. (I prefer vellum to the other options because it's sturdier and more transparent.)

- Lightbox (optional): A lightbox can be helpful for tracing outlines of your photo onto acetate and when assembling small pieces of your project.

- Acetate sheet protector to hold your photo as you trace (below), or inkjet transparency film if you prefer that method (page 33); both are available at office supply stores

- Thin permanent marking pen (I use Sharpie Ultra Fine Point) to trace photos onto acetate sheet protector

- Pencil and eraser for tracing projected image onto vellum or other paper

- Masking tape to secure acetate drawing or inkjet transparency to overhead projector plate or lightbox and to tape paper for master drawing to wall, if desired, instead of pinning

- Scotch tape (matte finish, ¾″ wide) to tape together paper for your master drawing if necessary

- Wall, foamcore board, or other hard surface to pin or tape paper and project the acetate drawing or inkjet transparency during enlargement

TRACING YOUR PHOTO ONTO ACETATE

The average 4″ × 6″ color photo is a bit small to work with, so enlarge your photo to approximately 7″ × 9″ (you can do this on your computer or have it done at a copy shop). (**Note:** The glass plate on an overhead projector is usually 10″ × 10″, so it's best to keep your acetate drawing smaller than these dimensions. Otherwise, the outer edges of your design won't be visible when you project the image.)

If you can see the values (lights and darks) clearly on your enlarged color photo, then you can use it to trace. If things look a bit mushy and you're unable to distinguish shapes, then it may be helpful to use a 7″ × 9″ black-and-white photo—it's often easier to discern values in shades of gray than in colors. You might even want to posterize your photo (page 29) to help distinguish values.

Place your 7″ × 9″ photo inside the sheet protector. Then trace the outlines with an Ultra Fine Point Sharpie, using a lightbox if necessary.

Trace your photo onto acetate.

As you trace, keep in mind that appliqué requires closed shapes, so make sure all your lines are connected. However, you can draw reference lines to help later on with quilting, perspective, or fabric direction. For example, you may want to draw lines showing the direction of your favorite kitty's fur, but you don't need to get too detailed.

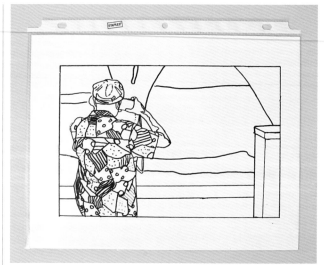

Completed acetate drawing (shown on a white background sheet for clarity)

Remember to draw straight lines around the perimeter of your photo. This will ensure that you work with shapes along the edges, while also indicating the outside boundaries when you project your drawing. These lines will also help you see if your projection is distorted so that you can adjust it before you trace (page 33).

You can also simplify your design at this stage if there's something you want to eliminate. If you're not sure, leave the original item in for now, even if you think you may substitute something else later on. That way, you'll have a better idea of the proper positioning and perspective for anything you might use in its stead.

MAKING AN INKJET TRANSPARENCY

Another way to transfer your photo for enlargement is to print the image on transparency film, using your computer and inkjet printer.

You can make the same adjustments (lighten, darken, posterize, etc.) to an inkjet transparency as you can to a photo; the only difference is that it's printed on transparency film rather than on paper. As with your original photo, a black-and-white transparency may work better than a color one.

Inkjet transparency

It's important that you use transparency film marked for use with an inkjet printer. Your printer will have at least one appropriate setting for inkjet transparency film.

As with an acetate drawing, keep your transparency smaller than 10″ × 10″ so that your design won't be too large for the projector's glass plate.

Sometimes, even after I've done the inkjet transparency and have started work on the master drawing, I find that I can't see something clearly enough. This is when I go back to the computer and enlarge a portion of the photo for clarity (page 28). Once I figure out the shape I need, I can resume the master drawing.

Enlarging Your Image

After you have completed your acetate drawing or inkjet transparency, it's time to enlarge the image for your master drawing. Using an overhead projector, the basic procedure is as follows:

1. Place your acetate drawing or inkjet transparency on the glass surface of the overhead projector.

2. Project your image onto a wall or other hard surface (foamcore works well) onto which you have pinned or taped paper large enough for the size of your drawing.

3. Move the projector forward or back until your image is the size you want. You may also need to adjust the focusing mechanism and the angle of the lamp, checking to make sure that the outer corners of the projected image are square.

4. Once your projected image is the size you want, use masking tape to hold the acetate drawing or inkjet transparency in place on the projector's glass surface. Trace the projected image onto the vellum or paper. I use pencil so that I can erase mistakes easily. Don't forget to include the straight lines around the perimeter of your image.

As you trace, you may notice areas you'd like to change. For me, these changes often involve simplifying the background. However, I usually draw the original elements to use as a placement guide for any substitutions I might make later on, just as I did with the original acetate drawing (pages 31–32).

SELECT YOUR FABRICS

Selecting fabrics for pictorial quilts can be fun and challenging at the same time. No matter what kind of fabrics you're looking for, you'll need to pay attention to color and scale, as well as the suitability of the prints themselves.

Although I have a fairly sizable stash, I often have to go in search of less "exciting" fabrics, such as beige for sand, to suit the needs of my current project. The problem with my stash is that it's filled with large colorful flowers, animal prints, and children's novelty fabrics that followed me to the cash register when I should have been looking for quiet solids or plaids. The good news is that I can always use the more exuberant fabrics I've collected on the backs of future quilts!

How Much to Buy?

If I see good water, sky, grass, stone, or wood fabric that might make up a large area of an unknown future quilt, I'll buy about 2 yards. For fabrics that I like but that are unlikely to take up a lot of space in a quilt (maybe they'd be suitable for purses, shoes, or hair), I'll usually buy ½ yard. And I like to have at least 1 yard of anything I might use to represent clothes.

Color

Because color frequently attracts me to a scene, I most often use the hues of the original photograph in my quilt. But you shouldn't be afraid to change colors if you think it will make the quilt more interesting—or if you just can't find the fabric you're looking for.

If you don't want to cut up your fabrics just yet, you can experiment with a computer graphics program to see how some elements of your photo will look in different colors.

Sometimes you just need to add a spot of color, as I've done with red geranium fabric in several quilts. I'm not sure this variety of geranium grows everywhere, but in my world, it grows wherever I need a little color. I've put these flowers on tables in France and poolside in New Mexico.

These red geraniums grow wherever I need a little color.

Small bits of color or brightness also help move the viewer's eye around the quilt. In *'52 Pickup* (page 25), your eye follows the yellow license plate, the red taillights, and the bits of silver in between.

Hand-dyed or painted fabrics and batiks are good for skies, though you should avoid cartoonish fabrics with evenly spaced white clouds (I sometimes call these fabrics "look at me" prints). Sky and water fabric are often interchangeable; if not, the right quilting design can do the trick. (Remember too that you can alter the color with quilting thread.)

Good sky fabrics

Too cartoonish for a realistic sky

It's a good idea to use several shades of green for foliage and grasses. After all, that is what Mother Nature does, and you can't go wrong emulating her!

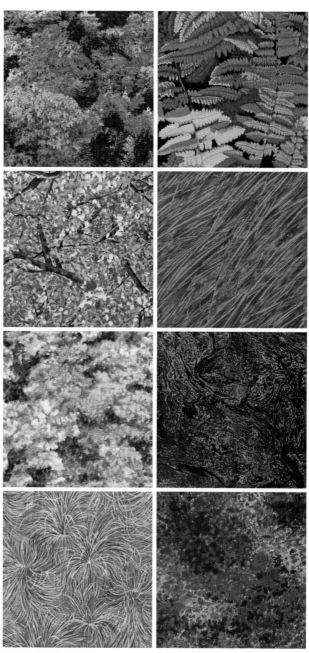

Some of Mother Nature's many colors and textures

The value, or lightness and darkness, of your colors is important as well. I talk about value on pages 65–66 when I cover how to achieve depth.

Scale

Scale is the relative size of the design on your fabric. You may have something in your stash that you think is perfect, but after you enlarge your drawing, you might realize that the pattern is not the proper scale. In *Ladies in Waiting* (page 71), several likely candidates were too large in scale for the finished size of the flowered dress, and I had to continue my search for the right fabric.

Rejected flower prints for *Ladies in Waiting*

Flowered dress in original photo

Flower print used in *Ladies in Waiting* (full quilt on page 71)

You also need to consider scale when you use architectural and nature-themed fabrics, such as bricks, stones, wood, bark, skies, water, foliage, and flowers.

Architectural fabrics of different scales

Wood and bark fabrics

Don't worry if you can't find fabric that's an exact match for an object in your photo. In fact, using something a little different can add a spark of interest to your quilt. The photos on page 38 show some colors and textures that could stand in for wood or bark as easily as the more realistic fabrics shown here.

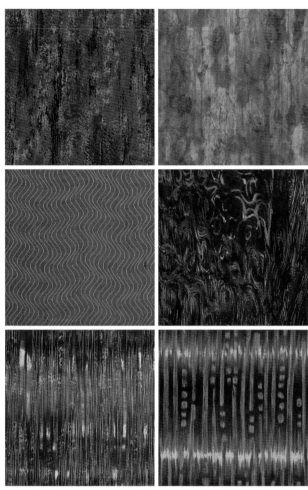

Alternative fabrics for bark or wood

Paper-pieced umbrellas in *Sidewalk Café* (full quilt on page 72)

Let the Fabric Do the Work

After you've been at this for a while, you'll begin to wise up and let the fabric do the work.

I used freezer paper to paper piece the umbrellas in *Sidewalk Café* (page 72) with individual black and white fabrics. By the time I did *Gone for a Dip* (page 73), however, I got smart and used striped fabrics of different widths for the chairs.

Striped fabrics in *Gone for a Dip* (full quilt on page 73)

In *French Laundry* (page 12), after I'd spent a lot of time on the purple shirt and the turquoise pants to get the shading just right with appliqué, I used a mottled commercial fabric for the green pants, which produced the desired effect with far less work.

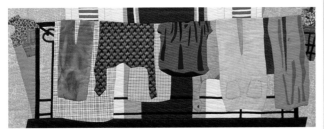

Clothes in *French Laundry* (full quilt on page 12)

Mottled fabrics are also quite useful for depicting flesh tones, as I did with *Ladies in Waiting* (page 71). I used a dark beige batik for the lady on the left and mottled prints in pink and peach for the other three.

Flesh tones in *Ladies in Waiting* (full quilt on page 71

If you're using a mottled fabric for flesh and need to make it a bit darker in a small spot, you can touch it up with a colored pencil.

When shopping for fabric, look beyond the obvious characteristics of a pattern to find what you need. A lion's mane in that wild jungle print might be perfect for a child's hair in your quilt. I used the same fabric for the wooden chair in *Front Row Seat* (page 62) as I did for the woman's hair in *Window Shopping* (page 26).

Wood grain fabric used to represent wood (full quilt on page 62)

Wood grain fabric used to represent hair (full quilt on page 26)

USE THE WRONG SIDE OF THE FABRIC

Another way to let the fabric do the work is to use the wrong side.

For *Ladies in Waiting* (page 71), I used the right side of the brown fabric for the darker bench seat and the wrong side for the lighter bench back. This ensured that both lighter and darker values were the proper hues. I also used the reverse side of the plaid for the lady on the right to represent the sunlit portion of her dress.

Using both sides of bench fabric (full quilt on page 71)

Using both sides of plaid fabric (full quilt on page 71)

The ladies at either end have hair of the same fabric, though it is treated a bit differently. I used the right (darker) side of the fabric for the lady on the left and placed the design on the bias. I used the wrong side of the same fabric for the lady on the right, with the pattern going straight up and down.

Right side of bias-cut fabric (full quilt on page 71)

Wrong side of straight-grain fabric (full quilt on page 71)

"FIX" YOUR FABRIC

Sometimes, however, the fabric is unable to do all the work. In that case, ask yourself whether quilting, embellishment, paints, or pencils might solve the problem later in the process. I don't embellish much in my own work, but on occasion it can be the perfect solution, and you should do whatever works for you.

In *Taos Pueblo* (page 74), I used quilting lines on the ladder to simulate wood grain fabric. In *French Shoes* (page 72), I used paint for the dots on the sides of the shoes and for the dots and other design elements on the straps.

Quilting lines simulate wood grain in *Taos Pueblo* (full quilt on page 74).

Painted designs in *French Shoes* (full quilt on page 72)

Using Tulle for Shadows

If I can't find fabric in just the right shade to represent a shadow, or if the reverse side of the same fabric doesn't work, I apply an overlay of *tulle*, a fine netting used in bridal gowns. It has also come in handy for the windows of cars and trucks. Tulle is available in many colors; you may need to experiment to see which color works best and whether you need more than one layer.

Often you can treat the tulle as a second layer and manipulate it together with the fabric underneath (for larger areas, I sometimes use a fabric adhesive spray to hold the tulle on top of the fabric). An example of this would be *'52 Pickup* (page 25), where I used tulle to shade the truck windows.

Tulle shading on truck windows (full quilt on page 25)

In *'52 Pickup*, I was able to hide the ends of the tulle in the seams. But sometimes you'll need to lay the tulle on the fabric with all edges exposed, as I did in *Front Row Seat* (page 62) for the shadow behind the chair.

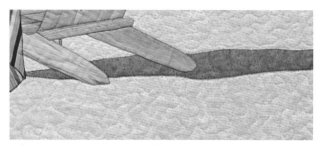

Tulle shadow placed directly on fabric (full quilt on page 62)

Here's how to prepare the tulle for direct placement on fabric, using a freezer-paper template as your stitching guide. See page 47 for full instructions on making a freezer-paper template.

1. Cut a freezer-paper template the shape you need for the shadow.

2. With a hot, dry iron, press the template shiny side down onto a piece of tulle, covered with a Teflon pressing sheet (otherwise your tulle will acquire many more holes!).

3. Pin the tulle to your fabric. Hand baste outside the edges of the template to hold the layers together and to ensure that the tulle lies flat. Remove the pins. If the template comes loose, press it again.

Freezer-paper template, tulle, and fabric layers

4. The freezer-paper template will now stay in place to serve as a guide. Stitch around it with a small straight stitch. I set my stitch length at about 1.5 and use an open-toed embroidery foot for visibility.

Experiment with stitch length and thread color to get the most unobtrusive results. You'll often be surprised at what works and what doesn't. I start with 60-weight thread (on the top and in the bobbin) that matches the tulle and/or the background fabric. If the colors you use at first don't work, try invisible thread on the top in clear or smoke.

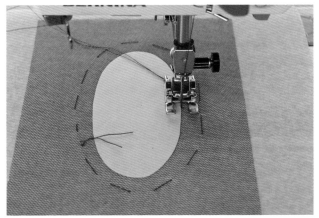

Stitching around the template (contrasting thread used for visibility)

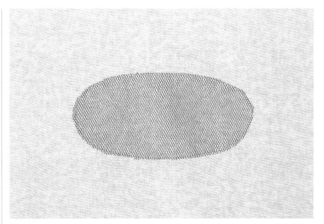

Finished shadow: The top thread matches the fabric, and the bobbin thread is slightly darker.

5. Remove the freezer paper and the basting.

6. With small, sharp scissors held parallel to the fabric, carefully cut away the excess tulle outside the stitching. You may need to go around the piece more than once to get close enough to the stitches. Give the piece a final press covered with a Teflon pressing sheet.

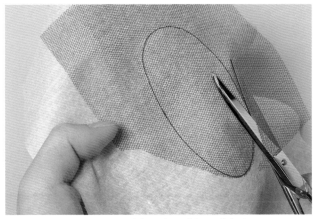

Cutting away excess tulle (red thread used for visibility)

OTHER SPECIAL FABRICS

Organza (silk or polyester) also works well with the methods described for tulle. I especially like using organza to represent the milky look of reflections in windows. For small metallic pieces, such as automobile door handles, I like to use lamé. Mistyfuse, a light-weight fusible webbing, works well for fusible appliqué with tulle, organza, and lamé. If you'd rather not fuse, you can use tricot-backed lamé. For an example of this, see the bumpers in *Mama's Got a New Set o' Wheels* (page 15).

When working with special fabrics and threads, it's a good idea to note your machine settings so you can duplicate the process on future quilts without reinventing the wheel. I keep a small notebook for this purpose.

Quiltmaking Tools and Supplies

Since I don't work in a very large space, I try to make up for it by using the best possible tools and supplies. Regardless of space, this is a good practice for anyone to follow.

Sewing machine: The projects in this book require a sewing machine with a zigzag stitch. Some of the projects also require a darning foot and the ability to lower or cover the feed dogs.

You could use the regular foot that comes with your machine for the machine appliqué zigzag stitch, but an open-toed embroidery foot allows you to see your stitches better and makes it easier for you to achieve the desired results.

When you are ready to quilt, lower or cover your feed dogs and use a darning foot for free-motion quilting or a walking foot if you have decided to quilt in straight lines.

Left to right: Open-toed embroidery foot, darning foot, walking foot

Needles and thread: The following needles and threads are used for the projects in this book. (I like using cotton thread and Schmetz Microtex Sharp needles.)

- 60-wt thread with #60/8 sharp needle
- 50-wt thread with #80/12 sharp needle
- 50-wt thread with #70/10 sharp needle
- Invisible thread (clear or smoke) on the top and 50- or 60-wt thread in the bobbin, with the needle size corresponding to the bobbin thread weight
- White thread and hand-sewing needle for basting

Note: These are all three-ply threads. Some 50-weight threads are two-ply, and you can use those in place of a 60-weight three-ply thread.

Additional tools and supplies:

- Rotary mat, cutter, and ruler
- Pins
- Seam ripper
- Scissors for paper and fabric
- Freezer paper to make templates for turn-under and raw-edge appliqué
- Cuticle stick or That Purple Thang from Little Foot, Ltd for removing freezer-paper templates from appliqué pieces
- Gluestick to affix raw-edge appliqué pieces to background
- Wax-free transfer paper (such as Saral, available at art supply stores) to transfer your design to background fabric, if desired

- If you fuse: Wonder-Under or your favorite brand of paper-backed fusible web and Teflon pressing sheet(s) to protect your iron and ironing surface
- Design wall (foamcore board covered with batting, felt, or Pellon fleece)
- Steam iron and fairly hard ironing surface
- Batting (I like the thinner cotton varieties, such as Quilters Dream Cotton in Select or Request loft.)

Optional:

- Clover mini iron to press the seams of your appliqué pieces onto the shiny side of freezer-paper templates (You can do this with a regular iron [no steam], but the mini iron makes it much easier.)
- Stiletto to hold down turned-under fabric edges as you guide your pieces through the sewing machine (or you can use a seam ripper)
- Dritz Fray Check, applied with a wooden toothpick (comes in handy if your fabric starts to fray)
- Muslin base, depending on your method of working (page 62 for guidance)
- Small digital camera to help with fabric choices

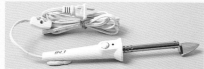

Clover mini iron

MACHINE APPLIQUÉ THREE WAYS

Now that you have prepared your master drawing (page 30), it's time to learn the various methods of machine appliqué. I will talk about turn-under, fused, and raw-edge appliqué. Once you've worked through the exercises in this chapter, you can develop your skills further with the three projects at the end of the book.

The Right Choice for the Job

A quilt show judge once commented that my quilt was nice, but it was too bad I hadn't used the same technique all the way through. I assume she was referring to the way I turned under some edges and fused others. My response is that had I not fused those tiny pieces, I'd still be working on that quilt! So I say that you should feel free to mix and match techniques to your heart's content and do whatever you need to get the job done. Each method will produce a different look in the final product, so it's important to use the one that will give you the desired results with the least difficulty. Here are some guidelines for when to use each of the three techniques.

Turn-under appliqué: Although this method is the most demanding of the three, I like the way it looks and use it as much as I can, unless there's a better reason to do it another way. It has a clean, sharp edge, and the stitches practically disappear into the quilt, allowing the fabric to take center stage. It works well with my simple graphic style, and it has the added advantage of nicely surviving multiple rip-outs, a feature not to be underestimated!

Fused appliqué: Fusible web is a good choice when the pieces are tiny or intricately shaped and you still want a clean edge. And if you are more interested in product than process, fusing can help you reach that goal, particularly if time is short.

Raw-edge appliqué: If you don't like the extra stiffness of fusibles, raw-edge appliqué works well for delicate subjects, such as flowers and hair. In this method, you cut fabric shapes (either freehand or with a freezer-paper template), glue them to the background, and straight stitch close to the edges.

Turn-Under Appliqué

This technique uses a machine zigzag stitch. Before you get started, you'll need to set up your machine.

MACHINE ZIGZAG STITCH

For zigzag appliqué, the settings listed at the right work for my Bernina 1260. Your own machine may require different settings, so use these guidelines as a starting point and make adjustments until you achieve the desired results.

Whenever possible, I try to use 60-weight thread with turned-under edges, because it is the most unobtrusive. However, since not all local quilt shops carry it, I have included settings for the more familiar 50-weight thread as well. Your stitches will show up a bit more with the 50-weight, but you'll still get a nice result.

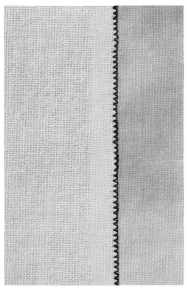

Detail of zigzag appliqué stitches with 60-weight thread (dark thread used for clarity)

Machine Settings for Zigzag Stitch Appliqué

For 60-Weight Thread

- *Matching or contrasting 60-wt thread in top and bobbin*
- *Top tension 3*
- *Bobbin thread through hole in bobbin case finger, if your machine has one, to tighten the bobbin tension*
- *Stitch width 1*
- *Stitch length .75*
- *#60/8 sharp needle*
- *Open-toed embroidery foot (Bernina #20)*

For 50-Weight Thread

- *Matching or contrasting 50-wt thread in top and bobbin*
- *Top tension 3*
- *Bobbin thread through hole in bobbin case finger, if your machine has one, to tighten the bobbin tension*
- *Stitch width 1.25*
- *Stitch length 1*
- *#80/12 sharp needle*
- *Open-toed embroidery foot (Bernina #20)*

A few words regarding thread choice: If you want your stitching to blend in as much as possible with your background, use thread that matches your appliqué piece in both the top and bobbin. If you can't find matching thread, use invisible thread on top (clear for lighter colors and smoke for darker ones) and thread to match the background fabric in the bobbin.

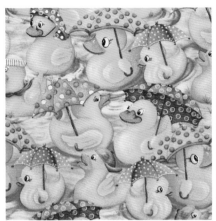

Rubber Ducky Exercise

This little rubber ducky appliqué exercise includes the inner and outer curves and points that you are likely to encounter in your own designs. Use this simple pattern to practice the turn-under machine appliqué techniques.

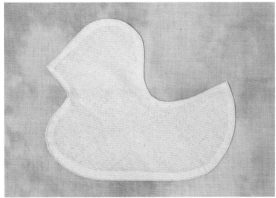

Rubber Ducky practice piece

MATERIALS

In addition to the general supplies listed on page 44, you will need the following:

- 6″ × 6″ fabric square for the duck

- 7″ × 7″ contrasting background fabric

- 6″ × 5″ piece of freezer paper

- 60-wt thread to match the duck fabric (If 60-wt thread is unavailable, use 50-wt thread and adjust your machine settings as described in Machine Zigzag Stitch on page 46.)

- Clover mini iron (optional)

PREPARE THE FREEZER-PAPER TEMPLATE AND FABRIC

1. Place your freezer paper shiny side down over the rubber ducky pattern (page 48).

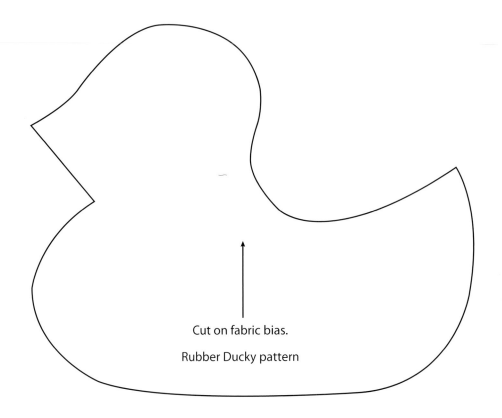

Cut on fabric bias.

Rubber Ducky pattern

2. Trace the pattern onto the freezer paper. I use a pencil so I can erase mistakes easily. If desired, use a ruler along the bottom of the duck and along the straight edge of its beak. Transfer the arrow to the freezer paper to help you orient the piece on the fabric later.

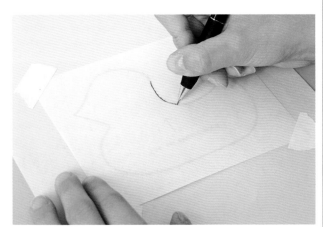

Trace the pattern onto freezer paper.

3. Cut the freezer paper piece along the traced line. This is your template. I use 5″ scissors for more control, though this is a matter of personal preference.

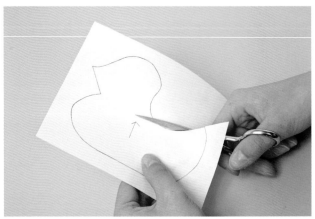

Cut the template from freezer paper.

4. With a hot, dry iron, press the freezer paper template *shiny side down* onto the *right side* of your fabric. Position the template arrow at a 45° angle so your fabric is on the bias. Glide the iron over the fabric once or twice; there is no need to press too hard, since your iron is hot.

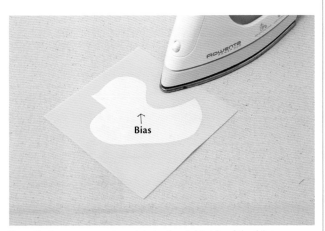

Press the freezer-paper template to the right side of the fabric.

Prewashed fabric sticks more easily to freezer paper.

Cutting small curved pieces on the bias makes it easier to turn under the curved edges and minimizes fraying.

5. Cut the fabric around the template, leaving a scant ¼″ seam allowance.

Cut fabric around the template.

6. Clip the inner curve and the inner point of the beak so they will lie flat. There is no need to clip the outer curves.

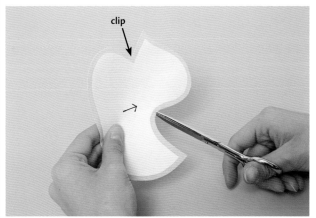

Clip inner curve and inner point of beak.

If your fabric starts to fray, particularly at the inner point below the beak, use a wooden toothpick to apply a tiny dab of gluestick or a drop of Fray Check. (If your fabric is not tightly woven, you may want to do this as a preventive measure before you clip the seam allowance.) Be careful to stay within the seam allowance, because Fray Check will darken and stiffen your fabric.

TURN THE EDGES

For additional tips, see Troubleshooting Points and Curves *(page 51).*

1. Now that you have established the outer boundaries of your appliqué piece, gently pull off the freezer-paper template and place it *shiny side up* on the *wrong side* of the fabric. Make sure your seam allowance is even all around.

I prefer not to pin the template to the fabric in the usual manner, because it won't lie perfectly flat. If necessary, I'll place the template and fabric on the ironing board and insert a few pins vertically to hold everything in place temporarily.

Freezer-paper template, shiny side up, on the the wrong side of the fabric

2. Turn and press the ¼″ seam allowance onto the shiny side of the freezer paper. Sometimes it's easier if you first press 2 opposite sides (in this case, the top of the duck's head and the straight edge along the bottom); you can then remove the pins and make your way around the remaining edges with your iron.

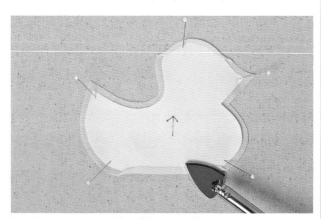

Pressing two opposite sides of the seam allowance

It's easier to press the seam allowance on an ironing board that isn't too thickly padded.

I use a Clover mini iron set on high. If you don't have a mini iron, make sure your regular iron is dry, because the steam can burn your fingers. You can also protect

your fingers by using a stiletto or cuticle stick to hold the seam allowance as you press.

You can use a heavy mug to hold the mini iron between pressings.

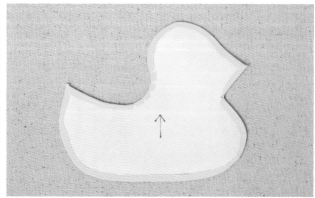

Pressed seam allowance

3. Gently unstick the pressed seam allowance from the freezer paper with a cuticle stick or That Purple Thang, and carefully remove the freezer paper.

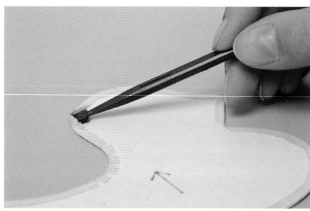

Unstick the seam allowance.

You may want to line the duck if you think a dark background will show through (even if you cut out the background from behind, sometimes the seam allowances will remain dark). With the same or other light or white fabric, cut a second duck shape from the template, without seam allowances, and slip it beneath the turned-under edges of the duck.

4. Hand baste the seam allowance (through the lining if you've added one; see the tip on page 50) with a light-colored contrasting thread, making sure your stitches aren't too close to the folded edge so as not to interfere with your machine stitching. It's also best to keep your stitches fairly short.

To make it easier to pull out the basting after you machine appliqué, keep the beginning and ending thread ends on the right side of the piece and don't make a knot at the end.

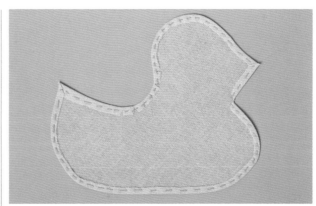
Hand-basted seam allowance (contrasting thread used for visibility)

5. Give the piece a final pressing.

Troubleshooting Points and Curves

Here are some things to watch for as you work your way around the duck.

Outer curves: *If you get points and wrinkles as you press the outer curves, your seam allowance is too wide. Gently lift the seam allowance with a cuticle stick or That Purple Thang, trim it, and press it back down. Sharp curves require more trimming than gentle ones, so your seam allowances may not be even all the way around. I don't worry about this as long as the piece looks good from the right side.*

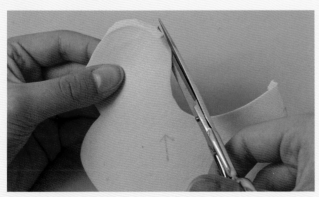
Trimming too-wide seam allowance (arrow on freezer paper is showing through fabric)

Outer points: *When you fold the upper edge of the tail to form a point, you'll need to trim the excess fabric hanging over the edge. This will also happen when you press the seam allowances that form the outer point of the beak.*

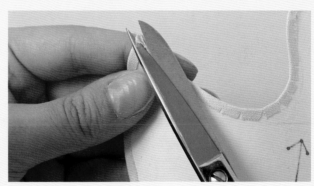
Clip excess fabric from outer points.

Inner curve: *If the inner curve doesn't fold over readily, you'll need to clip more and/or farther in. For best results, use sharp scissors that cut at the tip of the blades.*

Inner point: *If you have trouble turning under the inner point below the beak, make sure the freezer paper and fabric are aligned properly. If realignment doesn't help, you may need to clip farther into the seam allowance with sharp scissors.*

STITCH THE APPLIQUÉ TO THE BACKGROUND

1. Pin and hand baste the duck to the background fabric. You can use longer stitches than you did to baste the seam allowance. Remove the pins. Since this was a small piece, I basted around the edges; with larger work, I'll sometimes baste a big X across the piece.

Baste the piece to background fabric (red thread used for visibility)

I like to use a lighter thread (usually white) to baste down the seams and a darker one (usually gray or beige) to baste the appliqué piece to the background fabric. That way, if I baste a piece to the quilt and later decide to move it, I won't inadvertently remove the seam allowance basting.

2. Machine appliqué the duck onto the background fabric, starting at Point A. Read through Stitching Techniques at right before you start.

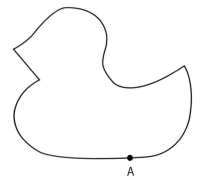

A

Start stitching at Point A.

3. When you're done machine stitching, remove all the basting stitches. Cut out any excess background fabric from behind the appliqué, ¼″ inside your stitching. Steam press on the wrong side.

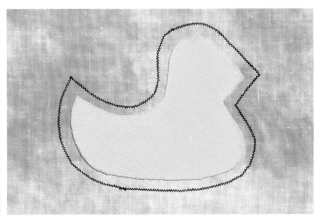

Carefully cut away the background fabric (contrasting thread used for visibility).

STITCHING TECHNIQUES

Here are some tips to help you with the straight edges, curves, and points that you'll encounter when you machine appliqué. Contrasting thread is used in the photos for better visibility.

Starting to stitch: I usually find it easiest to start stitching along a straight edge or, if none is available, a gentle curve. To start, bring your bobbin thread to the top through the background fabric, just outside the folded edge of the appliqué, and take four or five tiny (about 0.5mm) straight stitches. When it's convenient, clip the threads.

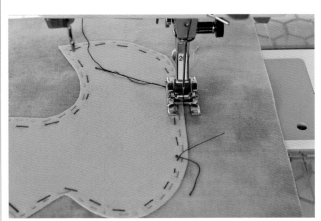

Initial straight stitches

Straight edges: To start your zigzag stitch, change settings as indicated on page 46. The goal is a nice neat stitch that will hold the piece securely, while remaining fairly unobtrusive. Guide your fabric so that the folded edge of the appliqué feeds under the needle in a straight line, parallel to the presser foot toe. As your needle swings to the left, it should jut over the fold and into the appliqué piece. When it swings back out to the right, it should pierce the background fabric just outside the fold. For more control, you may want to use a stiletto or seam ripper to hold down the folded edge as you stitch.

Guiding fabric along a straight edge

If you have trouble guiding your fabric straight, you can set your needle position to the far right for both straight and zigzag stitches if your machine allows. Stitch along the folded edge just inside the right toe of the presser foot.

Avoid the temptation to stitch too fast along a straight edge; this can lead to a marathon rip-out session (ask me how I know!). That said, if you do have to rip out, this method survives it pretty well.

Outer curves: As you approach an outer curve, the folded edge of the appliqué will start to feed toward the needle on an angle, signaling that it's time to pivot.

Pivot when the fabric starts to feed on an angle.

With the needle down in the background fabric, lift the presser foot, turn the fabric so the edge of the appliqué is once again parallel to the presser foot toe, and resume stitching.

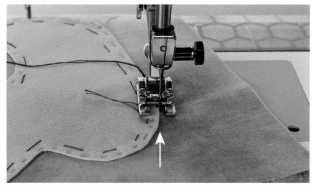

Fabric position after pivoting

Inner curves: As you approach an inner curve, your fabric will start to angle, as it did with the outer curve, but from the opposite direction.

The procedure is the same as with outer curves, except that when you pivot, you want your needle down in the appliqué rather than in the background fabric. Once again, make sure the edge of the appliqué is parallel to the presser foot toe when you resume stitching.

On long gentle curves, you won't need to pivot much, if at all. Instead, you can move your fabric as you stitch (slowly!) to ensure even stitches. Just remember to feed your fabric straight under the needle as you stitch.

Outer points: Stitch until your needle pierces the background fabric at the very edge of the point. Lift your presser foot and pivot so that you are ready to stitch the next side. Lower the presser foot and resume stitching. Your first stitch will enter the appliqué and overlap the previous stitches from the first side, creating a securely stitched corner.

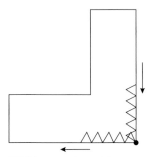

Stitching an outer point

Inner points: When you reach an inner point, let your needle make an extra stitch or two to equal the stitch width. Stop with your needle down and to the left in the appliqué. Lift the presser foot, pivot, and resume stitching down the second edge (your first stitch will swing to the right). Your stitches will overlap in the corner.

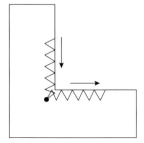

Stitching an inner point

Here's an easy way to remember where your needle should be when you pivot: On *outer* curves and points, pivot when your needle is on the *outside* of the appliqué. On *inner* curves and points, pivot when your needle is on the *inside* of the appliqué.

Ending your stitching: Once you've worked your way around the appliqué, zigzag over the initial straight stitches as well as a few of the first zigzag stitches. Then take four or five tiny straight stitches over the next few zigzag stitches. Clip the threads.

Fused and Raw-Edge Appliqué

Fused appliqué yields quick results with clean edges, while raw-edge appliqué is great for textured effects.

Palm Tree Exercise

This palm tree is a good subject for practicing both fused (the trunk) and raw-edge appliqué (the fronds).

Palm Tree

MATERIALS

In addition to the general supplies listed on page 44, you will need the following.

- Tree trunk: 4″ × 7″ brown fabric

- Palm fronds: 6″ × 6″ square of green fabric

- Background: 6″ × 9″ contrasting fabric

- Paper-backed fusible web for the trunk: 4″ × 7″ (I use Wonder-Under.)

- Freezer paper for the fronds: 6″ × 5″

- 50-wt thread to match your fabrics*

- Gluestick

I prefer 50-weight thread to 60-weight when I fuse, because it does a better job of covering the raw edges.

MAKE THE TRUNK: FUSED APPLIQUÉ

Note: *When you work with paper-backed fusible web, your drawing needs to be reversed.*

Follow the manufacturer's instructions for working with your fusible web.

1. Place the fusible web paper side up over the trunk pattern at right and trace with a pencil. The trunk has been reversed for tracing.

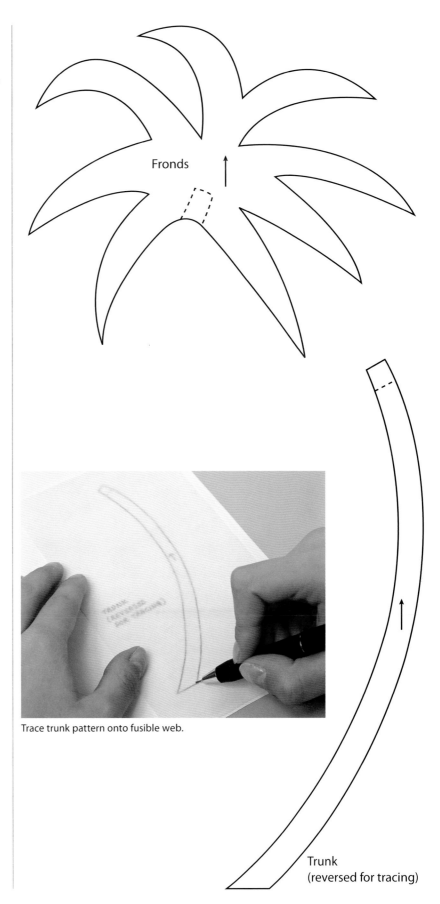

Trace trunk pattern onto fusible web.

Fronds

Trunk
(reversed for tracing)

2. Press the fusible web to the wrong side of the brown fabric, using the arrow to position the pattern as desired on the fabric. (For example, I placed the trunk fabric with the lines running across the trunk, perpendicular to the arrow on the pattern piece.)

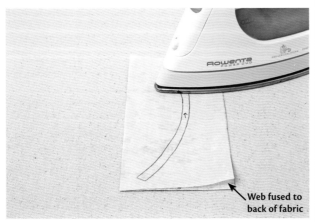

Web fused to back of fabric

Fuse the web with the drawing to the wrong side of fabric.

3. Cut the trunk on the line. Gently remove the paper backing and place the trunk glue side down on the background fabric. Make sure the bottom of the trunk is straight across and parallel with the bottom edge of the background fabric—if you were to temporarily place the pattern piece back on the trunk, the arrow would point up. Allow enough room at the top for the palm fronds. Press.

Iron the trunk to the background fabric.

4. Stitch the trunk to the background. Refer to Machine Settings for Fused Appliqué below to set up your machine.

Machine Settings for Fused Appliqué

These settings are a guide; test them on your own machine and make adjustments if necessary. See page 54 for instructions on stitching outer points.

- *50-wt thread to match your trunk fabric in top and bobbin*

- *Top tension 3*

- *Bobbin thread through hole in bobbin case finger, if your machine has one, to tighten the bobbin tension*

- *Stitch width 1.5*

- *Stitch length 1*

- *#70/10 sharp needle*

- *Open-toed embroidery foot (Bernina #20)*

5. Starting at the top right corner of the trunk, bring up your bobbin thread and take 4 or 5 tiny (about 0.5mm) straight stitches in the background fabric.

6. Switch to a zigzag stitch, work your way around the trunk to about ¼″ before the end of the top left corner, and end with 4 or 5 tiny straight stitches. You do not need to stitch across the top of the trunk, because the fronds will overlap it. Clip threads and steam press on the wrong side.

You are now ready to prepare the palm fronds and practice raw-edge machine appliqué.

MAKE THE PALM FRONDS: RAW-EDGE APPLIQUÉ

1. With a pencil, trace the palm frond pattern (page 55), including the arrow, onto the dull side of your freezer paper.

2. Place the freezer-paper drawing dull side up onto the right side of your green fabric, with the arrow pointing up. Press with a hot, dry iron.

3. Cut out the freezer paper and fabric together on the line.

Cut freezer paper and fabric on line.

4. Peel off the freezer paper.

5. Dab gluestick on the back of the fabric and place the fronds over the trunk above the zigzag stitches, using the dashed lines on the pattern pieces on page 55 to aid in placement if needed.

6. Free-motion straight stitch close to the edges of the fronds. Refer to Machine Settings for Raw-Edge Appliqué below to set up your machine.

Machine Settings for Raw-Edge Appliqué

- *50-wt thread to match your palm frond fabric in top and bobbin*
- *Top tension 2*
- *Stitch width 0*
- *Stitch length 0*
- *#70/10 sharp needle*
- *Darning foot*
- *Lowered feed dogs or covered throat plate*

Raw-edge appliqué, with its frayed edges, is particularly useful for objects found in nature, such as flowers and leaves. If the edges are more ragged than you'd like, stitch closer to the perimeter and trim any raveled threads. You can also stitch the edges down more securely when you quilt.

QUILT TOP ASSEMBLY

Now that you know how to create your appliqué pieces, it's time to put them together. Whenever possible, I like to assemble my pieces into units before placing them onto the quilt background (page 59).

How you put your quilt top together will depend on the appliqué method(s) you use and whether you're working in units from foreground to background or vice versa, as described below.

Planning and Preparation

Once you've created a master drawing and selected your fabrics, you can prepare your templates and fabric as shown on pages 45–57. You may want to review The Right Choice for the Job (page 45) to help determine which appliqué method(s) will work best for your project, keeping in mind the following additional guidelines.

OVERLAPPING PIECES

Your quilt is likely to contain some pieces that overlap, and you'll need to plan ahead for those. For turned-under edges, mark small x's on your templates along any edge that will underlap another piece. This reminds you later to leave a seam allowance of ½″ or more along that edge.

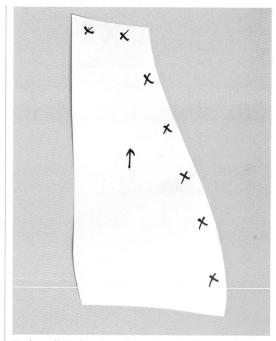

Mark small x's along template edge to indicate underlap.

Unlike turned-under edges, fused edges require just a ¼″ underlap, as shown in the Palm Tree exercise (page 54), where the raw-edged palm fronds overlap the fused trunk. The smaller underlap prevents excess bulk (this also works when both pieces are fused).

I don't worry about specific underlap measurements for raw-edge quilts. In this more freeform style, you can place your fabrics just about anywhere you want. If you miss a spot, you can lightly glue another piece right over it—without fusibles or turned-under edges, the fabric won't bulk up too fast.

OUTER QUILT EDGES

Leave an inch or two of extra fabric around the perimeter of your quilt so you can trim it later without cutting into the design. This is easy to remember when you're working with one large background piece, but you might forget if you're working with smaller pieces at the outer edges of your quilt. Small x's at the edge of those templates will remind you to leave extra fabric.

Constructing Your Quilt

Because most of my work is fairly large, I prefer not to cut out all the templates at once—I'd rather not have to keep track of them all at the same time. Instead, I trace my freezer-paper templates, one at a time, from the master drawing on my design wall. (You can work flat on a table if you prefer, but be sure to use a design wall at some point in the process. It really does help you see how your work is developing, particularly with landscapes.) I then build up the quilt in units as described at right, using the master drawing as a guide.

When you draw your templates, be sure to mark each piece with an arrow to help you remember which way is "up." The arrow will also help you orient your piece for fussy cutting or fabric grain (on the bias, for example).

I like to start with whatever area of the design interests or amuses me the most. When my quilts contain figures, I begin with the clothing. For automobiles, I may start with a taillight or a wheel. In *Sidewalk Café* (page 72), I started with the umbrellas. If I get stuck on one element, I work on another part of the quilt for a while before tackling the original problem again. A solution usually presents itself the second or third time around. Sometimes you just have to be patient.

WORKING IN UNITS: FROM FOREGROUND TO BACKGROUND

Since my main subjects are often large, solid shapes—and because I don't usually know what my background will be—I like to construct them individually from smaller units and put them on a background later. Let's use *Drumming Up Business* as an example.

Drumming Up Business

In this quilt, everything was turn-under appliqué except the foreground flowers, which were raw-edged. As I finished portions of the gondoliers, I pinned them to the master drawing on the design wall.

1. I worked on the pants first, because they were simple shapes and large enough to give me a sense of progress early on.

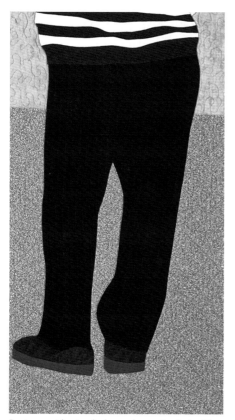

Pants provide simple, large shapes to start with.

2. I then worked on the heads, hair, and hats, but I could just as easily have worked on the shirts. I hand basted the ears and hair to the heads to create units to attach to the hats on one side and to the shirts on the other.

Hand baste units together far enough from the turned-under edge so you can temporarily lift or fold up the edge and machine appliqué the beginning or end of any piece that goes underneath it.

Folding up an edge to machine appliqué underneath: The green thread holds the turned-under edges, the red thread holds the light piece to the dark piece, and the yellow thread holds the two-piece unit to the background.

3. I machine embroidered cloth, with stabilizer underneath, to create fabric for the straw hats. I basted the ribbon shapes onto the hats, letting the long ends hang free for the time being, and then basted the assembled hats to the heads.

The head and hat form a unit to attach to the shirt.

Although it may be tempting to machine appliqué within the units, it's usually best to wait, unless you're certain that your stitching won't interfere with anything you do later. For example, if I had machine appliquéd the collar of the left gondolier to his head, I wouldn't have had a clean, unbroken line of stitching along the top edge of the collar when I later stitched the entire piece to the background fabric.

4. Next up were the shirts and hands, followed by the shoes. For the shirts, I appliquéd the dark stripes onto a large white piece of fabric, using my freezer-paper templates as a guide, instead of fussing with narrow pieces in two colors.

5. Once the individual units were assembled, I basted them together so I would have two fully formed gondoliers to put on the background.

Placing Units on the Background

After constructing my simplified background and appliquéing the windows and flower stand (putting them together in units as with the gondoliers), I added the figures, as described below.

1. With the background in place on the design wall, I pinned the master drawing along the top edge, making sure it lined up with the flower stand.

2. I slipped the gondoliers into place under the master drawing and pinned them flat against the background, checking against the drawing and moving them as needed. The semitransparency of the vellum makes it especially suitable for this purpose.

3. Once I was satisfied that the gondoliers were in the right spot, I was ready to pin, baste, and machine appliqué them to the background.

WORKING IN UNITS: FROM BACKGROUND TO FOREGROUND

Sometimes, however, it makes more sense to work from background to foreground. One example is *Gone for a Walk* (page 73), where the background shows through the chairs.

Gone for a Walk was worked from background to foreground.

In this case, it was easier to put fragile pieces such as chair arms and legs into place on a background with a traced design, as described below, than to slip them under a vellum overlay as I did in *Drumming Up Business* (page 60). If you haven't chosen a background yet, you can also work this way with a temporary muslin base (page 62).

Tracing Your Design onto a Background

1. Pin the background (either single-fabric or constructed) onto your design wall.

2. Pin your master drawing over the background along the top edge.

3. To transfer the drawing, slip a piece of wax-free transfer paper, coated side down, between the drawing and the background. Use a ballpoint pen to trace the lines of your drawing onto the background. Vellum holds up well to this process.

4. Keep moving the transfer paper around until you've traced the entire design.

You are now ready to pin, baste, and machine appliqué your prepared pieces to the background. I like to assemble my pieces into units as much as I can before stitching them onto a background (page 59). However, you can work directly on the background with individual pieces if you prefer, as long as you keep in mind which pieces overlap as you work.

Landscapes

Because the background is an integral part of any landscape, it makes more sense to work from background to foreground, layering each successive element as you go. Using your master drawing as a guide, you might start with a piece of sky fabric, for example, and appliqué or piece mountains, water, and sand in sequence as you move forward, creating the background. Then you might add rocks, beach chairs, or umbrellas in the foreground. *Front Row Seat* is a good example of this technique.

Front Row Seat inspiration

Front Row Seat, 36˝ × 25˝, Marcia Stein, 2005

You can use the vellum overlay method (page 61) to guide you in the placement of your foreground pieces; or, once you've created your background, you can use wax-free transfer paper to trace foreground elements from your drawing (page 61). Use whichever method you prefer.

Do You Need a Muslin Base?

There are several reasons for using a muslin base when working from background to foreground. (To make a muslin base, follow the instructions on page 61 for tracing a design onto a constructed or single-fabric background.)

If you plan to fuse or use raw-edge appliqué for all elements of your design, you can use a muslin base that will remain a permanent part of the quilt.

If you're using turned-under pieces that have gaps where the background will show through—such as the bench in *Ladies in Waiting* (page 71)—but you haven't yet chosen a background, you can use a temporary muslin base, as I did, to help place your pieces in the right spot as you go along. Once I had assembled all the ladies and basted them onto the bench, it was easy enough to remove the muslin from behind and place the entire basted unit down on the real background, using the vellum overlay method (page 61). (I didn't want to keep the muslin in the quilt because it would have made it too heavy.)

Sometimes it's handy to fuse small elements of your project onto muslin and then appliqué the larger piece onto the background. Examples of this might be flowers for a window box or small pieces of fabric used to represent shaggy dog hair.

MAKING CHANGES ALONG THE WAY

Your master drawing isn't written in stone, and you should feel free to make changes at any time as you assemble your quilt.

Changing Basic Elements

Note: Although I most often make the following types of changes to the background, you can use the same principles to change any of your main figures or other foreground elements.

As I mentioned in Combining Photos (page 26), sometimes you'll want to use another photo to help change a background, as I did in *Window Shopping* (page 26). Now that you know more about the technical aspects of making your quilt, I'll show you how I used my photo of a shop window in Florence, Italy, to simplify the jumbled background of the inspiration photo.

Shop window in Florence, Italy

I knew right away that I would have to change the bright yellow jacket to something less obtrusive in my quilt. I also had to take up more space than one item could fill. My original idea was to have five dresses in the window, but that proved to be too many. Here's what I did.

1. I made an acetate tracing from my photo that I projected and traced onto freezer paper. This created an appropriately sized template for all the dresses. As I drew, I eliminated the sleeves and lengthened the jacket into a dress.

2. I then made five tracings of the template onto the vellum drawing of the couple. For two of the five positions, I flipped the template so it would face the other direction. Ultimately, I used only three dresses in the quilt, fashioning a dress stand for the one on the right.

Master drawing with five dresses (detail)

If your addition is more straightforward than mine, you can project and trace directly onto your original master drawing, rather than making templates.

3. Eliminating two dresses and leaving the other three in place didn't work, so I spent quite a bit of time positioning the remaining dresses into a pleasing arrangement. I especially wanted to make sure the dresses didn't "grow" from the top of anyone's head. Once I settled on an arrangement, I made a freezer-paper template for the dress on the right so it would be properly oriented for turning under the edges.

4. I auditioned a number of black-and-white fabrics and discovered that subtle color differences (rich black vs. charcoal, cream vs. white) had more impact than I'd anticipated.

Rejected black-and-white fabrics

Window Shopping (detail; full quilt on page 26)

Once I was happy with the dresses, I chose a subtle print background that would contrast with the dresses and not compete with the couple.

Help from Your Digital Camera

There you are, working merrily along on your design, when something starts to nag at you, but you can't quite put your finger on it. This is where your digital camera, with its ability to provide instant feedback, is invaluable.

We see in three dimensions with our two eyes, while a camera captures only two dimensions with its one lens. Our memory of a scene includes not only the sight but also the sound, touch, taste, and scent of the moment, whereas a camera merely records the light. But although the camera's literal recording can sometimes make us unhappy with our photos because they don't look like the original scene, it can work to our advantage in the studio when it highlights design errors in our quilts.

A camera is particularly useful for seeing that blob or two of white (or yellow or silver) that catches your eye and stops it from moving around the quilt. This is how I discovered it would be best not to give white shoes to any of the *Ladies in Waiting* (page 71)—in fabric (more than in the original photo), the result was a bit too "look at me." Conversely, a camera can also alert you if you need a little more white in other areas of a quilt to balance things out.

Your camera is also a good tool for testing alternatives as you work, especially for backgrounds and foregrounds: Blue sky or fence? Sand or grass? Street or wall? A photo can tell you immediately if any of your fabric choices are off the mark in color, value, scale, or contrast. Your camera's not just for birthday snapshots anymore!

How to Achieve Depth

People often ask me how I achieve depth in my quilts. The easy answer is that I try to follow what's in the photograph. This means that I consider depth when I'm taking pictures, long before my fabric goes up on the design wall.

But what if we're not successful in achieving the illusion of depth when we take a photograph? The good news is that when we go from photo to fabric, we can remedy the situation by following some of the same principles.

Here are some ways to achieve the illusion of depth:

- Overlapping objects makes it obvious to the viewer that the item in front is closer, regardless of its size. An example of this would be a still life with an apple in front of a pitcher.

- Objects that are closer to us appear larger, so adding something to your foreground can improve the illusion of depth. This is why you'll sometimes see landscape photos with rocks or flowers in the foreground, leading you into a scene.

- Parallel lines that appear to converge in the distance convey a sense of depth. Railroad tracks are a good example of this.

- Emphasize the relative size of a group of similar objects. In this photo, the horses and riders in the distance appear smaller than the ones that are closer to us.

Using relative size to show depth

- Include shadows and highlights. I've been known to disregard this guideline on occasion if I'm going for a more graphic look. That said, it's always good to be aware of your intentions and know why you're breaking a "rule."

- Pay attention to value. You need both lights and darks to create the shapes that give the illusion of depth. If you want something to appear closer, make it darker. As objects get farther away, they appear lighter and less detailed. For example, distant objects outdoors can take on a bluish cast.

- Use the properties of color. Warm colors (red, orange, yellow) advance, while cool colors (blue, green, violet) recede. So if your photo of a woman in a blue dress on a green background looks a little flat, try changing her clothes to a warm color to bring her forward and enhance the illusion of depth.

- Frame your scene in the foreground. Branches, doorways, and arches are often used for this purpose.

You can also accomplish some of these illusions of depth when you quilt. Heavier quilting in an area will cause it to recede, lighter or darker thread can change the value of the fabric, and puffier batting will give more dimension to your quilt.

Adding Design Elements

I've talked about simplifying designs, which is my usual bent, but sometimes I find it necessary to add a design element here or there. Most often it's because I need a spot of color. In several cases, flowers have done the trick. Other times, it's just because the quilt "needs something there."

In *Front Row Seat* (page 62), I added a colorful towel.

Detail of the original photo

Front Row Seat detail (full quilt on page 62)

In *All Dressed Up with No Place to Go* (page 73), I gave the figures necklaces. The mannequins in the original photo didn't need jewelry because they had that line where their heads swiveled off. When I translated them into cloth, however, they looked a little bare, so I had to figure out a way to compensate for that.

Detail of the original photo

All Dressed Up with No Place to Go detail (full quilt on page 73)
Photo by Marcia Stein

Not all of my attempts at jewelry were successful. I thought I might decorate my *Ladies in Waiting* (page 71) with earrings, but after a few hours' work with nothing more to show for it than a design wall littered with tiny circles and ovals, I decided to leave their ears alone.

I didn't realize until another visit to Santa Fe years later that the chairs in *Gone for a Dip* (page 73) were sitting in front of a parking garage (making my initial attempts to replicate the background all the more ridiculous!). But I still needed something more than a blank wall, so I inserted three windows, complete with colorful flowers, vases, and chili peppers.

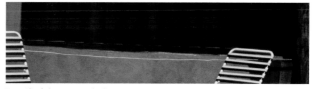
Detail of the original photo

Gone for a Dip detail (full quilt on page 73)

I added a vase to the windowsill in *Taos Pueblo* (page 74) for a bit of color and interest.

Detail of the original photo

Foreground detail of *Drumming Up Business* (full quilt on page 23); original photo (left) and quilt (right)

Taos Pueblo detail (full quilt on page 74)

Background detail of the original photo

Drumming Up Business background detail (full quilt on page 23)

Since I had eliminated the bright orange tablecloth in the background of the original photo (page 22), I found I needed a bit more color and interest in *Drumming Up Business* (page 23). I achieved this by adding a flower vase in the foreground and window boxes filled with flowers in the background.

So don't be afraid to change things here and there—it not only adds more interest to your work, but it's also fun!

FINISHING

Entire books have been written about quilting and binding, so I'll just say a few words about those topics here.

Quilting

Because my quilts are so graphic, I tend not to make machine quilting a major feature, unless it is used specifically to enhance the design. And though I don't often get ideas about how I'll quilt a piece until the time comes to actually do it, I tend to follow a similar procedure with each project.

First, I stitch in the ditch around the major shapes. If I quilt inside the shapes, I'll often follow their curves in parallel lines at regular intervals, using my walking or darning foot as a guide. Sometimes I follow the patterns in the fabric (stitching circles around stones or outlining flowers, for example). My later pieces are more heavily quilted than my earlier ones, because I learned the hard way that more quilting makes a quilt hang better. It also helps if you quilt evenly across the entire surface.

It's true that you shouldn't overlook problems in your appliqué or piecing with the idea that they will "quilt out." However, you can use quilting to strengthen your design by changing color with thread (don't forget to try different weights of thread, too) and by adding texture in places where you may not have been able to achieve the desired effect with fabric alone. You have nothing to lose by experimenting.

Bindings That Blend In

I like the bindings of my borderless quilts to blend in with the main design. This is easy enough to do if the seam joining two fabrics goes straight across. But sometimes the fabric needs to continue going on an angle through the binding, and this requires a slightly different approach.

You can use this procedure whether you have one long binding strip or four separate ones. I usually use one long double-fold strip, so that's what I'll demonstrate here. (If you use four separate strips, you can sew the joins as I describe before you attach the binding strips to the quilt.)

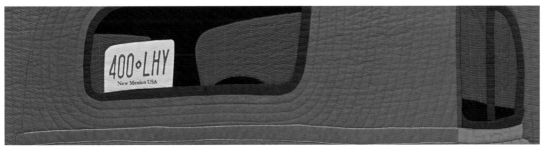

'52 Pickup quilting detail (full quilt on page 25)

1. Stop stitching about 6″ before the join. Backstitch a few stitches, clip your threads, and remove the quilt from the machine to make it easier to maneuver.

2. Fold the upper piece of binding (in this case, red) to the right, along what will become the ¼″ seam with the quilt. Mark the angle of the join with a marking pencil.

Mark the angle of the join.

3. Unfold the red binding and extend the mark to both edges. You will use this line as a guide for placement of the lower (blue) strip.

Extend the mark to both edges.

4. With the marking as a guide, fold the blue binding to match the angle of the join, keeping its side edges even with the red binding (a piece will stick out on the right side from underneath). Press the fold.

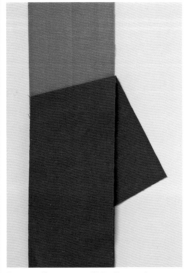

Proper alignment of binding strips

5. Unfold the blue strip and pin it to the red strip along the fold line.

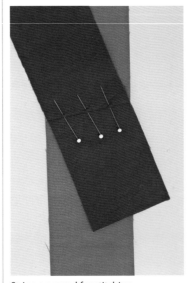

Strips prepared for stitching

6. Stitch along the fold. Trim excess fabric from underneath and press the seam open.

Sometimes it can be helpful to temporarily switch from a walking foot to an open-toed embroidery foot for better visibility when you stitch the joins.

7. Refold your binding to continue stitching it onto the quilt. Note that the join won't appear to be correct until the binding is turned to the back.

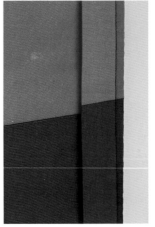

Binding before it is folded to the back

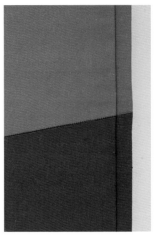

Binding after it is turned to the back

GALLERY

Ladies in Waiting, 67″ × 42″, Marcia Stein, 2004

Ladies in Waiting inspiration

Sidewalk Café inspiration

Sidewalk Café, 67″ × 43″, Marcia Stein, 1999

Monet's Garden inspiration

Monet's Garden, 31″ × 59″, Marcia Stein, 1999

French Shoes inspiration

French Shoes, 63″ × 48″, Marcia Stein, 1999

Gone for a Dip inspiration

Gone for a Dip, 63″ × 47″, Marcia Stein, 2000

All Dressed Up with No Place to Go inspiration

All Dressed Up with No Place to Go, 67″ × 47″, Marcia Stein, 1999
Photo by Marcia Stein

Gone for a Walk inspiration

Gone for a Walk, 71″ × 40″, Marcia Stein, 1999

Does Not Compute inspiration

Does Not Compute, 46˝ × 60˝, Marcia Stein, 1997
Photo by Marcia Stein

Taos Pueblo inspiration

Taos Pueblo, 40˝ × 45˝, Marcia Stein, 2000

Easily Distracted inspiration

Easily Distracted, 24″ × 39″, Marcia Stein, 2008

Goalll!!, 25″ × 28½″, Dorothy Foster, Alamo, CA, 2007

Flower Box, 25″ × 31½″, Jan Soules, Elk Grove, CA, 2009

Sisters, 27″ × 36″, Joan Bruce, Grover Beach, CA, 2009

Sisters, 34″ × 24″
Barbara E. Thorne, Huntington Beach, CA, 2009

McGinty Sisters Before Labor Day, 42″ × 31″
Sherry Davis Kleinman, Pacific Palisades, CA, 2007

Santa Fe Window, 9″ × 11″, Karen Flamme, Oakland, CA, 2006

Bathing Beauties . . . Yesterday, 33″ × 37½″
Carole Gentile, Pacific Palisades, CA, 2009

Puerto Vallarta Walk, 23½″ × 35″
Justine Lott, Santa Rosa, CA, 2009

A Durango Adventure, 28″ × 22″
Penny Youngflesh, Durango, CO, 2009

Cacti, 36″ × 24″, Judy Woodfill, San Francisco, CA, 2008

Casual in Kauai, 8¼″ × 11¼″, Nelda McComb, Jamul, CA, 2008

Brendan's '76 Saab, 31″ × 22″
Nancy Shepherd, Kansas City, MO, 2007

PROJECTS

FLOWER VASE

This project is a good way for you to develop your appliqué skills without having to enlarge a photo first. The full-size vase pattern is on page 82, and the flowers are fussy cut from fabric.

I used raw-edge appliqué for the flowers, because that allowed for a more detailed shape than I could get with turned-under edges. In contrast, I turned under the edges of the vase to give it the smooth, polished look of ceramic pottery.

To make the flowers, you may follow the pattern (page 81) or arrange them in a way that pleases you. Remember to add some greenery. Look at photos of floral arrangements or visit your local florist for ideas. I used the rule of thumb that says a vase and its flowers should be in equal proportion; another widely used guideline is that the flowers should never be less than one-third taller or more than two-thirds taller than the vase.

Fabric and Supplies

Use the general supplies listed on page 44. You will need an 8″ × 10″ piece of freezer paper for the vase template.

- **Vase:** 12″ × 12″ square of fabric that contrasts with your background and flowers (I chose something that resembled a vase I own.)

- **Flowers:** Assorted print fabrics with flowers of different colors and shapes that each measure approximately 2″–3″ in diameter

Flower Vase, 19″ × 24″, Marcia Stein, 2008

- **Leaves:** Scraps of green fabric (not solids, because they will appear too flat)*

- **Background:** ⅔ yard of fabric that contrasts with the flowers and vase

- **Backing:** ¾ yard

- **Batting:** 23″ × 28″

- **Binding:** ⅓ yard

- **Thread:**

    60-wt thread to match the vase fabric (If 60-wt thread is unavailable, use 50-wt thread and adjust machine settings accordingly [see Machine Zigzag Stitch, page 46].)

    Invisible thread to machine baste flowers and leaves to the background, if necessary

    Quilting thread of your choice

- **Notions:** Gluestick

You can use fabric with leaves that are about 2″–3″ long, or you can cut out leaf shapes of that size from textured fabric, such as batiks, hand-dyes, mottled, or tone-on-tone. Make sure your greens vary in size and color, just as they do in nature.

Prepare the Vase

See Turn-Under Appliqué *(pages 46–54) for complete instructions on template preparation and turning the edges.*

1. Make a freezer-paper template of the full-size vase pattern (page 82). Mark small x's along the top edge to remind you to cut a larger seam allowance to extend underneath the flowers. Remember to transfer the arrow to your template.

2. With a hot, dry iron, press the template shiny side down onto the right side of your fabric. Point the arrow at a 45° angle so your fabric is on the bias. Remember to fussy cut if you have motifs that you want to appear on specific areas of the vase.

3. Cut the fabric around the template with a scant ¼″ seam allowance, but use a ½″ seam allowance along the top, where the edges of the vase will disappear underneath the flowers.

4. If necessary, clip inner curves so they will lie flat; the vase has gentle curves, so you may not need to do this.

5. Gently pull the freezer paper off the fabric and place it *shiny side up* on the *wrong side* of the fabric, making sure the ¼" portions of the seam allowance are even all around.

6. Turn and press the ¼" seam allowance to the shiny side of the freezer paper, leaving the ½" seam allowance along the top unturned.

7. Gently unstick the pressed seam allowance from the freezer paper with a cuticle stick or That Purple Thang and carefully remove the freezer paper.

8. Hand baste the seam allowance and give the piece a final pressing if needed.

Machine Appliqué the Vase

See Turn-Under Appliqué *(pages 46–54) for complete instructions on machine appliqué with turned-under edges.*

1. Cut the background fabric to 21" × 26".

2. Hand baste the vase in place onto your background fabric.

3. Starting at the top right edge, machine appliqué around the vase with a small zigzag stitch, ending at the top left. I used white 60-wt thread to match the vase, but you may use contrasting thread if you wish. Remember to take 4 or 5 tiny straight stitches at the beginning and end of your stitching and to leave the ½" seam allowance free along the upper edge.

4. Remove all hand basting.

5. If you have a light fabric vase over a dark background, as I do here, you may want to carefully cut out the background fabric from behind the vase so that it doesn't show through.

Prepare the Flowers and Leaves

See Fused and Raw-Edge Appliqué *(pages 54–57) for complete instructions on raw-edge appliqué.*

1. Fussy cut the flowers from your fabric. Since flowered fabric often has few leaves, it's best to cut those separately from your leaf fabric. Use sharp scissors that cut to the tip. I prefer 5" scissors. However, because the cutting doesn't have to be precise, larger scissors may work fine for you.

2. Pin or glue the flowers and leaves to your background to hold them down temporarily, using the illustration (page 81) as a placement guide if you wish. If glue doesn't hold the flowers adequately for later quilting, baste them in place near their edges with free-motion machine stitching and invisible thread. When you quilt, you can use threads that match your flowers—your basting stitches will go unnoticed.

3. Turn the piece over and give it a quick steam on the wrong side.

Quilting

1. Layer and baste the top, batting, and backing.

2. Quilt in your favorite manner. I followed the lines of the flower petals with matching colors of decorative, shiny thread in the top and bobbin, leaving a few of the flower centers unstitched so they would puff up a bit to add dimension to the piece. As I went along, I made up vein patterns for the leaves, also in matching, shiny thread. I free-motion stitched around the design elements of the vase with white 60-weight thread so that it wouldn't stand out too much and detract from the simplicity of the vase design. Finally, I echo quilted around the vase and flowers with thread that matched the background.

3. Trim the quilt to 19″ × 24″ and bind using your preferred method.

Placement guide

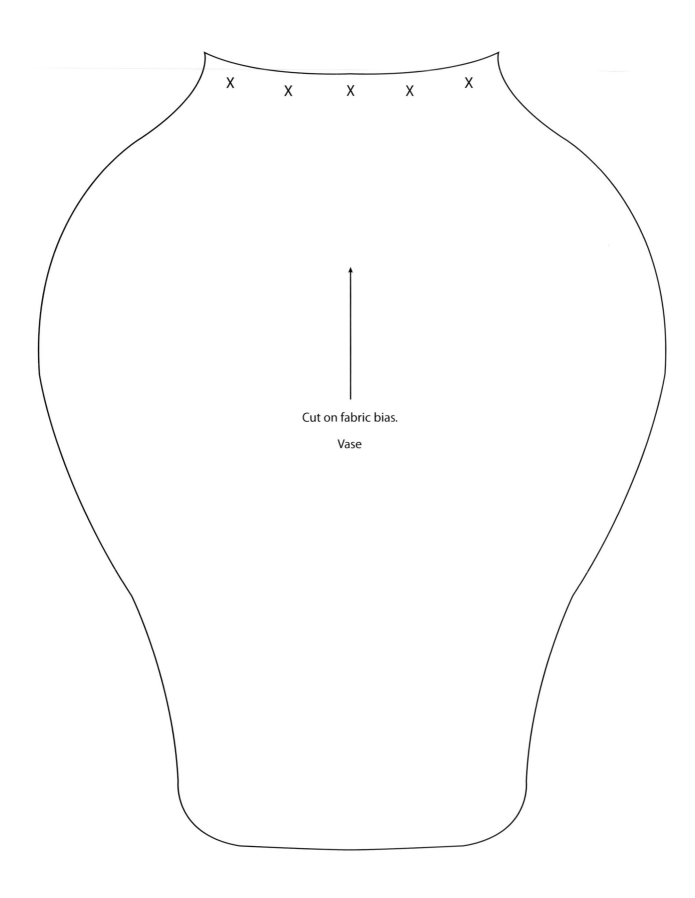

Cut on fabric bias.

Vase

SOCCER PLAYER

Soccer Player, 17″ × 26″, Marcia Stein, 2009

This little boy with the big soccer ball will walk you through the process of starting with a photo and ending with a quilt. I enlarged my drawing with an overhead projector, but you can create a piece the same size as the drawing (page 85) if you prefer. In the latter case, I recommend that you fuse at least the smallest pieces, if not all of them (see the instructions on pages 54–57). The following directions are for an enlarged version using turned-under edges.

Original photo

Revised photo

I revised the original photo in several ways to make the illustration shown on page 85. I enlarged the boy and cropped out excess foreground and background so he would remain the central focus. I eliminated the fence because I thought it a bit too overpowering and too labor intensive to make. I also wanted to encourage you to supply your own background.

Fabric and Supplies

Use the general supplies listed on page 44. Before you select your fabrics, see Audition Your Fabrics (page 86).

Once you enlarge your drawing to the desired size, determine how much fabric you need. I've listed the fabric requirements for my quilt, which measures 17″ × 26″. (**Note:** Depending on how your fabric is printed, you may need more than the quantities listed if you want your design to run in a certain direction.)

- **Clothing, flesh tones, and soccer ball:** Large fabric scraps (up to ¼ yard or a fat quarter each) in desired colors

- **Foreground:** ⅜ yard

- **Background:** ⅔ yard

- **Backing:** ¾ yard

- **Batting:** 21″ × 30″

- **Binding:** ¼ yard (If you want your binding to match the foreground and background fabrics, you'll need ⅛ yard foreground and ¼ yard background.)

- **Thread:**

  60-wt matching threads for machine appliqué (If 60-wt thread is unavailable, use 50-wt thread and adjust your machine settings accordingly [see Machine Zigzag Stitch on page 46].)*

  Quilting thread of your choice

I hand stitched the lines on the soccer ball with 40-wt black cotton thread, going over each line 6 times.

Soccer Player

Trace and Enlarge

See The Master Drawing *(pages 30–33) for complete instructions on enlarging the pattern illustration.*

1. Trace the illustration (page 85) onto an acetate sheet, using an Ultra Fine Point Sharpie (pages 31–32). If you prefer, photocopy the illustration and insert the copy in an acetate sheet protector before you trace. On the diagram, small x's indicate which portions go underneath other pieces.

2. Enlarge the drawing with an overhead projector (page 33). If you want a quilt about the same size as mine, note that the lower edge of my drawing as positioned on the glass plate was approximately 41″ from the wall on which the image was projected. Alternatively, you can have a copy shop enlarge your drawing for you.

Audition Your Fabrics

For this quilt, I generally followed my "let the fabric do the work" philosophy. The wood grain fabric gives a lighter feel to the background, and I found a nice pebbled gray for the foreground. Mottled flesh tones help give dimension to the arm, legs, and face, and a mottled brown gives the dusty look of scuffed footwear to the shoes.

Since the boy was the most important part of the scene, I chose his fabrics first and made sure the ones I picked later for the foreground and background worked well with them. I used mottled fabrics for his shoes, shorts, and flesh tones, as well as for parts of his shirt and the yellow areas of the soccer ball. The hat includes a lighter shade of red for the top portion and for a small piece at the lower left. The soccer ball uses a lighter shade of yellow for highlighting at the top, and the left pant leg is darker than the right.

Note that I didn't try to copy the boy's original outfit exactly. Although I kept his clothes blue, the striped shorts of the original are now a darker mottled blue, the camouflage hat has turned to red, his sandals have become closed shoes, and he now has red socks. I encourage you to make whatever changes you like as well.

You can substitute, for example, a blue sky for the background and grass for the foreground. In fact, those were my original plans. But once I decided on blue for the outfit, I needed a contrasting color for the background, and the lighter wood grain fabric worked better for that. Similarly, once I made the foreground gray pebbles instead of grass, I had to switch the shoes from gray to brown. Your first choices are never written in stone, so don't be afraid to try different things until something works. (For more information about selecting fabric, see Select Your Fabrics on page 34.)

If you've decided on your foreground and background fabrics, you can sew them together now with a ¼″ seam and press toward the foreground. Otherwise, go ahead and start on the toddler, as I did. I suggest you start with the simpler shapes (face, legs, arm, shorts, socks, and shoes) before moving on to the shirt, hat, and soccer ball.

Prepare the Units for the Boy

Follow the instructions on pages 46–51 to prepare your templates and fabric for turn-under appliqué. You'll then baste the pieces together for placement on the background in one unit (pages 59–61). To ensure unbroken stitching lines, do most of the machine appliqué after the boy is completely assembled and basted onto the background.

Trace your freezer-paper templates from the master drawing. I do these one at a time. Remember to mark an arrow pointing up to assist you in orienting your finished pieces and to mark small x's at edges that will go underneath other pieces so you remember to cut a larger seam allowance in those areas.

1. Prepare the face/neck and arm.

2. Prepare the legs and baste them together, right leg over left, from the top to the point where they cross.

3. Prepare the 2 sections of the shorts and baste them together with the right (lighter) side on top. Machine appliqué the center seam using thread that matches the lighter piece.

> If you can't find fabric that you like for the darker section of the shorts, you can overlay a piece of tulle that's a bit larger all around. Fold the tulle and seam allowances under as one; then pin and baste.

4. Prepare the socks and shoes. Baste the socks to the legs and the shoes to the socks.

5. Prepare the light and medium blue pieces of the shirt, but don't turn under the lower edges yet. Baste and machine appliqué the medium blue piece to the light blue piece. Remove the basting and trim any excess fabric from behind. Turn under and baste the lower edge of the shirt.

6. Prepare the sleeve and baste it to the arm. Baste the sleeve/arm unit to the shirt.

Add the Soccer Ball

1. Prepare the dark yellow portion of the soccer ball. Then prepare the 4 hexagons and the yellow highlight piece and baste them in place. Machine appliqué the highlight and the 2 right-hand hexagons. Remove the basting from the highlight and trim any excess fabric underneath. Use your freezer-paper template to get a sharp turned-under edge for the top of the highlight; baste. Remove the basting from the 2 hexagons; there is no need to trim the fabric underneath.

> If you prefer, you can fuse the hexagons (see Fused and Raw-Edge Appliqué on page 54).

2. Position the arm/shirt in place on the soccer ball (a lightbox is helpful for this). Pin and baste.

3. Machine appliqué the 2 remaining hexagons. Remove the basting.

Finish the Boy

1. Prepare the 2 pieces that make up the lower tier of the hat. Baste the smaller piece to the larger one and machine appliqué the folded edge. Remove the basting and trim any excess fabric underneath. Fold and baste the outer edge of the small piece.

2. Prepare the top and middle hat pieces; baste and machine appliqué the top piece to the middle one. Remove the basting and trim any excess fabric underneath. Use freezer-paper templates to turn under the remaining outside edges of the hat; baste.

3. Baste the hat to the face/neck piece prepared earlier.

4. Baste the shirt to the neck.

5. Baste the lower edge of the shirt over the shorts.

6. Baste the lower edge of the shorts over the legs.

Assemble the Quilt

See Constructing Your Quilt *(pages 58–62) for complete instructions on assembling and placing units on a background.*

1. If you haven't done so already, sew your foreground and background together with a ¼″ seam and press toward the foreground. If you haven't yet decided on a background, now is the time to audition fabrics. Having your subject basted together can make this process easier.

2. Pin and baste the boy in place on your background. You can baste an X over the larger portions if you like, rather than going all around the edges.

3. Machine appliqué with thread that matches your pieces (pages 52–54). As long as you basted the boy securely to the background, you can start stitching anywhere you wish. I usually begin with major interior lines before working my way down to the smaller elements and outer edges. You may want to work with one color thread as long as you can before moving on to another area. Trim excess fabric from behind.

4. Layer and baste the top, batting, and backing.

5. Quilt in your favorite manner. I followed the lines of the wood grain fabric in matching thread and then quilted circles on the pebbled foreground. I stitched along the curves of most of the clothes and the soccer ball at regular intervals.

6. Trim the quilt to 17″ × 26″ and bind using your preferred method.

SMART CAR

Smart Car, 32″ × 23″, Marcia Stein, 2009

This little car will give you plenty of opportunity to further develop your skills. I enlarged my drawing with an overhead projector, but you can create a piece the same size as the drawing on page 93 if you prefer. In the latter case, I recommend that you fuse at least the smallest pieces, if not all of them (see the instructions on pages 54–57). The following directions are for an enlarged version. I turned under most edges, though I did fuse some small pieces as noted. You may wish to fuse other relatively small pieces, such as the taillights, as well.

Revisions to the Photo

As you can see from the original photo, I changed the silver piece on the side to black, because I prefer the look of the cars I've seen that way. If yellow doesn't appeal to you for the rest of the car, feel free to change the color. I also simplified the background.

Original photo

Since the car owner was unaware of my photography, I didn't want to use a real license plate. The one I used, 2GAT123, is a common fake number used in movies and television, so feel free to use it, substitute your own, or leave it out altogether.

Fabric and Supplies

In addition to the general supplies listed on page 44, you'll need a few other notions, listed below.

Once you enlarge your drawing to the desired size, determine how much fabric you need. Here are the fabric requirements for my quilt, which measures 32″ × 23″.

- **Car:**

  ⅝ yard of medium bright yellow fabric for car body (I used a mottled fabric.)

  ¼ yard of light yellow for highlights

  12″ × 3″ of sandy gold color for Piece C

⅓ yard of black for various pieces

Black tulle: 12″ × 5″ for back window; 10″ × 8″ for front window; 28″ × 5″ for shadows beneath car

Scraps of red for taillights and brake light

Scraps of light gray for taillights, tiny door light, and side mirror

Scrap of dark gray for door handle

Scrap of white (or color of your choice) for license plate

¼ yard of dark gray (a fat quarter would also work) and small amounts of light gray, medium gray, and black for tires

- **Foreground:** ½ yard of gray fabric for asphalt

- **Background:** ½ yard of blue sky fabric

- **Backing:** ⅞ yard

- **Batting:** 36″ × 27″

- **Binding:** ⅓ yard (If you want your binding to match your background and foreground fabrics, you'll need ¼ yard of each.)

- **Thread:**

  60-wt matching threads for turn-under appliqué (If 60-wt thread is unavailable, use 50-wt thread and adjust your machine settings accordingly [see Machine Zigzag Stitch on page 46]).

  50-wt matching threads for fused appliqué using paper-backed fusible web

  Quilting thread of your choice

- **Notions:**

  Silver pen for "smart" lettering on the trunk and the dot in the center of the hubcap

  Permanent fabric markers in appropriate colors for license plate lettering

  Colored pencil for license plate sticker

  Fusible web for smallest pieces

- **Optional:** Instead of black fabric for the steering wheel, I used ¼″ Clover bias tape. You can also make your own tape with a 6mm Clover tape maker.

Trace and Enlarge

See The Master Drawing *(pages 30–33) for complete instructions on enlarging the pattern illustration.*

1. Trace the illustration (page 93) onto an acetate sheet, using an Ultra Fine Point Sharpie (pages 31–32). If you prefer, photocopy the illustration and insert the copy in an acetate sheet protector before you trace. On the diagram, small x's indicate which portions go underneath other pieces.

2. Enlarge the drawing with an overhead projector (page 33). If you want a quilt about the same size as mine, note that the line at the lower edge of my drawing as positioned on the glass plate was approximately 43″ from the wall on which the image was projected. Alternatively, you can have a copy shop enlarge your drawing for you. (In either case, you may need to adjust the size of the license plate illustration on page 92 to fit your master drawing.)

Prepare the Units

Prepare your templates and fabric following the instructions for Turn-Under Appliqué (pages 46–54) and, when necessary, for Fused and Raw-Edge Appliqué (pages 54–57). You'll then baste the pieces together for placement on the background in one unit (pages 59–61). To ensure unbroken stitching lines, do most of the machine appliqué after the car is assembled and basted onto the background.

Trace your freezer-paper templates from the master drawing. I do these one at a time. Remember to mark an arrow pointing up to assist you in orienting your finished pieces and to mark small x's at edges that will go underneath other pieces so you remember to cut a larger seam allowance in those areas. Some pieces have been designated with a letter for convenience.

LEFT REAR PANEL

Prepare taillights, light yellow highlight (rear fender), and small black vent; machine appliqué or fuse to the left rear panel.

RIGHT REAR PANEL

Prepare and baste or fuse taillights in place on the right rear panel (they will hang over the outside edge). Do not machine appliqué them yet.

CENTER BACK PANEL

1. Before you put the trunk together with its adjacent pieces, print the "smart" logo with a silver pen on Piece A. Practice first on a scrap of the same fabric.

> Iron the fabric to freezer paper to make it easier to write on.

2. Prepare the license plate from the illustration on page 92, and machine appliqué it to the trunk. I traced the letters and numbers with fabric markers (a lightbox is helpful for this), and I used a colored pencil for the sticker in the upper right corner.

3. Prepare the light yellow highlight and machine appliqué it in place above the license plate. (I used a darker thread along the lower edge to add a slight shadow effect.)

4. Prepare Pieces B, C, and D. Machine appliqué the lower edge of B to C and the upper edge of D to C.

5. Prepare and fuse 2 small black dots to Piece E. (**Note:** When fused pieces are this tiny, I don't try to stitch around them; you can decide for yourself which fused pieces are worth the effort.)

6. Machine appliqué assembled Piece BCD to A at the top and to E at the bottom to complete the center back panel.

7. Machine appliqué the left and right rear panels to the center back. I used black thread to accentuate the lines.

DOOR AND FRONT

1. With light gray fabric, prepare and fuse the tiny light to the side of the door.

2. Prepare and machine appliqué the lower edge of the light yellow highlight along the top of the door, hood, and front fender.

3. Prepare the door handle and baste it in place on the door. (I fused the narrow black handle to the dark gray piece, and then fused this unit to the larger turned-edge black piece to complete the handle unit.)

4. Prepare Piece F and baste it in place over the lower edge of the door. Stop basting when you reach the top of the door handle.

5. Prepare Piece H and baste it in place under Piece F at the top and to the door at the bottom.

6. Prepare Piece G (the black triangular piece behind the side view mirror) and machine appliqué it under the thin strip of Piece F. Baste Piece FG under the top of the door.

7. Prepare the side view mirror and baste it in place over Piece FG. (I fused the light gray piece to the larger turned-edge black piece to complete the unit.)

WINDOWS AND STEERING WHEEL

1. Prepare the rear window frame and machine appliqué the brake light in place at the top. Trim any excess black fabric from behind the light. Fold the brake light seam allowance over the top of the window frame and baste it in place.

2. Place tulle underneath both window openings and baste in place.

3. Pin and baste the steering wheel in place behind the tulle. If you did not use prepared bias tape and instead

basted the seam allowances of your steering wheel, remove the seam allowance basting now. Otherwise, it will be impossible to remove it from behind the tulle once the background is in place.

REAR SECTION

1. Position and baste the right rear tire underneath the lower rear bumper edge. Then machine appliqué the unit over the center back and rear panels of the car.

2. Baste the rear window frame to the car and machine appliqué it in place over the center back and rear panels of the car.

LEFT REAR WHEEL

1. Prepare Piece K (the black oval that goes under the spokes) and machine appliqué it to Piece J (medium gray).

2. Fuse Piece L (the spoke hubcap) to assembled Piece JK; machine appliqué around the spokes, if desired.

3. Machine appliqué Piece M (tire) over Piece JKL.

4. Fuse the small black piece to the center of the hubcap. (I used a silver pen to make the dot.)

5. Baste the wheel unit to Piece N (wheel well). Baste the wheel/N unit to the left rear panel of the car.

6. Prepare Piece P and baste it over the wheel/N unit and under the body of the car.

License plate (resize if necessary)

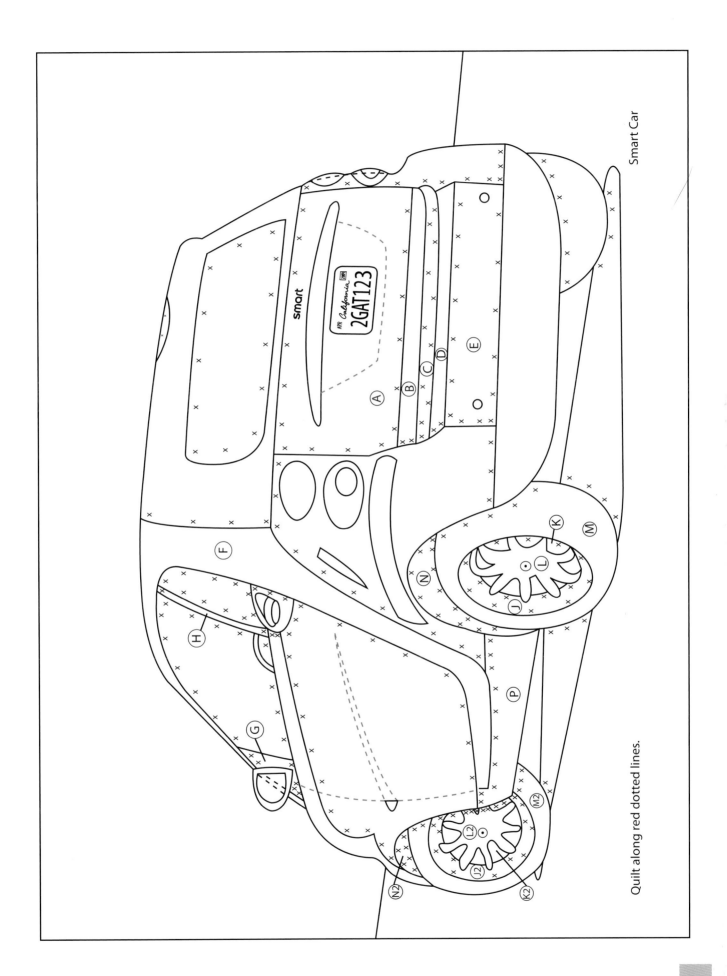

Smart Car

Quilt along red dotted lines.

7. Baste and machine appliqué the lower and right edges of Piece F to Piece P and the rear section of the car.

LEFT FRONT WHEEL

The left front wheel is assembled the same way as the left rear wheel.

1. Prepare Piece K2 and machine appliqué it to Piece J2.

2. Fuse Piece L2 to assembled Piece J2K2; machine appliqué around the spokes, if desired.

3. Machine appliqué Piece M2 (tire) over Piece J2K2L2.

4. Fuse the small black piece to the center of the hubcap. (I used a silver pen to make the dot.)

5. Baste the wheel unit to Piece N2 (wheel well); baste the wheel/N2 unit to the car.

6. Machine appliqué the front and rear fenders over the wheel units with thread that matches the car body.

You are now ready to create the background.

Assemble the Quilt

1. Machine appliqué or seam the foreground to the background. If you sew rather than appliqué, press the seam toward the foreground.

2. Pin the car in place on your background. Pin and baste tulle under the car for the shadows. Some of the tulle can be hidden beneath the tires; stitch the remaining tulle in place (pages 42–43).

3. Baste the car to the background. You can baste an X over the larger portions if you like, rather than going all around the edges.

4. Machine appliqué with thread that matches your pieces (pages 52–54). As long as you basted the car securely to the background, you can start stitching anywhere you like. I usually begin with major interior lines before working my way down to the smaller elements and outer edges. If you've followed the steps, many of the smaller elements and interior parts have already been appliquéd. You may want to work with one color thread as long as you can before moving on to another area. Trim excess fabric from behind.

Be careful when moving tulle under your needle so that it doesn't catch and tear. It's also a good idea to remove any jewelry that might snag the tulle as you stitch.

5. Layer and baste the top, batting, and backing.

6. Quilt in your favorite manner to add definition to the finished design. I quilted minimally, mainly stitching in the ditch around the major elements, but you can certainly do more if you like. I also quilted along the red dotted lines on the door and center back panel in the illustration (page 93). I used black thread for the vertical line on the front door to make the door shape obvious and to provide a nice balance to the black appliqué lines on the center back panel. Conversely, since the horizontal lines on the door and the detail around the license plate represent indentations on the car, I used thread that was slightly darker than the car body for more subtlety.

7. Trim the quilt to 32″ × 23″ and bind using your preferred method.

ABOUT THE AUTHOR

Marcia Stein is a San Francisco textile artist whose award-winning work has been shown in a number of juried exhibitions at galleries, museums, and quilt shows throughout the country and is included in several public and private collections.

Marcia's recent designs combine her interest in photography with her quilt art. She is currently at work on a series of pieces based on her photographs from Santa Fe, Italy, England, and the south of France.

Originally from Chicago, Marcia is a graduate of the University of Michigan in Ann Arbor. She took up quilting in 1992, after a lifelong interest in other needle arts, and has been pursuing her interest in textile art full-time since 1996. She has been lecturing since 2003 and teaching since 2004. You can reach her through her website at www.marciastein.com.

Great Titles *from* C&T PUBLISHING

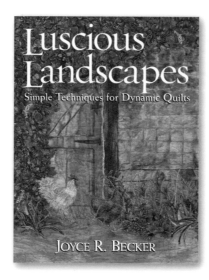

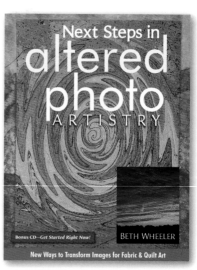

Available at your local retailer or **www.ctpub.com** *or* **800-284-1114**

For a list of other fine books from C&T Publishing, ask for a free catalog:

C&T PUBLISHING, INC.

P.O. Box 1456
Lafayette, CA 94549
800-284-1114

Email: ctinfo@ctpub.com
Website: www.ctpub.com

C&T Publishing's professional photography services are now available to the public. Visit us at www.ctmediaservices.com.

Tips and Techniques can be found at www.ctpub.com > Consumer Resources > Quiltmaking Basics: Tips & Techniques for Quiltmaking & More

For quilting supplies:

COTTON PATCH

1025 Brown Ave.
Lafayette, CA 94549
Store: 925-284-1177
Mail order: 925-283-7883

Email: CottonPa@aol.com
Website: www.quiltusa.com

Note: Fabrics used in the quilts shown may not be currently available, as fabric manufacturers keep most fabrics in print for only a short time.